LET THE DRUMS SPEAK!

The Story of Legendary Drummer

Bernard "Pretty" Purdie

Pretty Media, LLC

PO Box 200

Allenwood, NJ 08720

Copyright © 2021 by Bernard Purdie

All Rights Reserved

All rights reserved. No part of this book may be used or reproduced in any manner whatsoever, electronic, mechanical, photocopying, recording or otherwise, without the prior written permission of the publisher.

ISBN: 9798585309786

"Purdie was an innovator . . . the essential soul drummer . . . Purdie really built the sound of soul music in the sixties and in New York."

– Bob Porter, record producer

CONTENTS

ACKNOWLEDGMENTS AND DEDICATION
FOREWORD
INTRODUCTION   i

PART I. LEARNING TREE

1. BUGSY   1
2. RHYTHM PLANET   32
3. NIGHTCLUB COLLEGE   58

PART II. MAKIN' IT

4. NO LOOKING BACK   68
5. KING CURTIS   92
6. RHUBARB RED   103
7. SOUTH AFRICAN CONNECTION   112
8. THE DEMO KING   119
9. BOOGALOO BUGSY   128
10. PHILADELPHIA STORY   136
11. CHICAGO SOUL   148
12. JAZZ MASTER   151

13. MR. BIG SHOT   155

PART III. TURNING POINT

14. ATLANTIC RECORDS   160
15. ARETHA FRANKLIN   166
16. SPIRIT IN THE DARK   177
17. HEAVY IS THE HEAD   197
18. STEELY WHO?   207
19. M. C. BUGSY   216
20. THE RINGO STARR CONTROVERSY   223

PART IV. THE PURDIE EFFECT

21. WHAT IS FUNK?   226
22. PURDIE WISDOM   230
23. THE PURDIE LEGACY   236
24. HOME AT LAST   239

PHOTOS

APPENDIX

END NOTES

ACKNOWLEDGMENTS AND DEDICATION

I give honor to God for the desire and the perseverance to finish this book. This book is also dedicated to the session musicians and section players everywhere, who work so hard out of love for their instruments and for the music. In my estimation, they are the real superstars of music. Of course, many thanks to those on the Purdie team who helped me tell the many stories that make up the Bernard Purdie story—especially my siblings, who were more than willing to tell me the unvarnished truth about growing up with Bugsy. Everything you revealed to me went into the writing of this book, even if you weren't quoted. I couldn't have done it without you.

I would like to thank all the friends and fans that made this book a reality through their love and support. We have tried to list everyone who helped below and on the following pages. Please forgive us if there is anyone we left out. A special thanks to Ed Dennis.

Peace and love,

Bernard "Pretty" Purdie

ASSOCIATE PUBLISHERS

Lance Avery

Robert Friedman

Wayne Masiello

Jaye and Gary Pogoda

Cheri Rogowsky

Bobbie & Barry Siegel

PATRONS

Aaltje J Po

Aj Epyx Productions

Akira Komaki

Aleksander Skjæveland Larsen

Alex Kluft

Alex Stephens

Angelique Parraga

Anthony Del Vecchio

Anthony Thompson

Barry Keys

Bill French

Bill Horn

Bob Rice

Bob's No Problem LLC

Bobby Boyd

Brian Miller

Bruce Silverman

Celia Thompson

Chiropractic Lane

Christopher M. Girardi

Clarke S. Rigsby

Cleon Cato

Colette Pesce

Constance Riess

Cyril Mckinnon

Dante & Maud Cogliano

Dariusz Sliwinski

David Lucas

Dawn Reshen-Doty

Deanne and Bill Chenitz

Debbie Schwartz Maciolek

Deborah Storke

Denis Schreiber

Dennis Chan

Delores Purdie

Don Lewis, Sr.

Doug Wilson

Dr. & Mrs. William R. Chenitz

Elliott Hinds

Francine Schneiderman

Francis Cicala

Gabriel Resende

Galt MacDermot

Gary Foster

Gayle Sokoloff

George Naha

Gerald Lane

Geraldo Magalhaes Melo Filho

Hana Dolgin

Harbans Srih

Hugh Mura

Ira Elliot

Jack & Yumiko Hoban

Jackie Pock

James Lewis

Jeffrey E Jacobson, Esq.

Jerald Gary

Jobst Upmeier

Joe Kroll

John A Criscuolo

John Anter

John Picetti

John Riddle

Joseph Calzone
Joseph Saccoccio
Jules Follett
Karen Frisk
Karsten Jeschkies
Kevin Mcintyre
Kristen Ritter
Kristi Sweeney
Lang Percussion Inc
Linda
Louis Paparozzi
Louis Wright
Mario Cicerello
Mark Rooney
Marshall & Margaret Johnson
Martha Chang
Matt Powell
Matthew Norris
Michael Chambers
Michiyo Menjo
Miho Nobuzane
Monica R
Morris Arnold Lang
Music Millennium

Nancy Yerrall Gale

Nando Pettinato

Nicole Thompson

Nirio Garcia

Pat Clark

Pat Floyd

Patricia & Curtis A Purdy

Patricia Purdy

Phyllis Purdie

Ric Schnupp

Richard T. Boyle

Rimbert

Robert Blumofe

Robert Del-Rose

Robert Levers

Robert Mccann

Roger Mclachlan

Russell Clarke

Samuel Elijah

Sandra & Rob Paparozzi

Sarah Partridge

Sharon May

Shiro Hara

Slim Chance & The Gamblers

Soundandimage

Stephanie Petaway-Hickson

Steve Bryant

Steven Abrams

Super Sassy

Tammy Martin

Taylor Tote Music

Tetsuya Sato

Tj Nelligan

Tone Heighton

Tyree Campbell

Wilson Zildjian

Foreword

by Bob Porter

It was 1969 and I was preparing to record Johnny "Hammond" Smith. We discussed the band and had agreed on everybody when Johnny said he'd like to use Bernard Purdie on drums. I knew of Purdie but had never met him. It sounded like a good idea.

For the session, Purdie arrived with a music stand containing a sign which said "Pretty Purdie – you done hired the hitmaker." The session was loose and three tunes came together on the date—there was no sheet music. One, a flat-out jam, was titled "Soul Talk" and Purdie cut loose with a drum solo which dominated the track to the point that we titled the album Soul Talk.

From this point forward, Purdie was my drummer. Over the next two years he played on sixteen albums for Prestige including two of his own, Purdie Good and Shaft. After I left Prestige, I tried to use him whenever possible and we remained good friends.

Apart from his style and obvious talent, what Purdie brings to a record date is his enthusiasm. He always brings his "A game" and never phones it in. He is like that in his personal appearances as well. He finds a way to make music work and for the listener to have a good time. *With Let The Drums Speak*, he tells you how he does it. Enjoy!

– Bob Porter is a producer, writer, and broadcaster. His book, Soul Jazz: Jazz In The Black Community, 1945-1975 will be published by Oxford University Press. He has been a radio host on WBGO since 1979.

INTRODUCTION

The International Music Products Association holds its summer trade show in Anaheim, California. With more than 1,300 exhibiters and 75,000 attendees, the exhibition causes the cavernous Anaheim Convention Center to pulsate with a cacophony of riffs from electric guitars, violins, drums, horns, pianos, and other instruments of every kind. Melodic lines float gently upward from a cello only to be scattered by a flight of screaming electric guitars. In the courtyard, thirty-five trombones meander through graceful Glenn Miller arrangements. The delicate violins ignore the din and refuse to be played, while the haughty pianos sit and observe in royal display beside their ever-watchful retinue of suited attendants. Anybody can whack a drum, so everybody gives it a try. A constant thunder rolls through the percussion section from the time it opens in the morning until it closes at night.

In a corner of the drum section, Bernard Purdie sits on the drum throne and plants his feet on the pedals. He adjusts the dampening gels on the drumheads, then looks up and smiles. He takes no notice of the racket all around him. Purdie begins to play—softly. The drumsticks glide imperceptibly over the batter head of the snare drum as the snares begin to sing. His massive left leg bounces lightly over the high hat's pedal, bringing it to life. His right foot awakens the bass drum, and its huge lung starts to breath. As Purdie plays, a crowd gathers before his drum kit. He doesn't seem to notice. His eyes are closed, his body undulating in a sensual dance. Purdie's expression is one of utter bliss. His audience has slowly grown three deep in the narrow aisle, heads bobbing with the gentle rhythm.

The surrounding clamor continues unabated, but within the orbit of his sound, Purdie has transported his audience to another place, leaving the sonic confusion behind. No longer is Purdie merely playing the drums; he's telling a story through ancient voices. His eyes are still closed. This is a séance. Spirits from before the dawn of history are being conjured. Purdie, in touch with these spirits, brings them forth at will and presents them for all to experience. Theirs is a language without words, a language of the purest energy. They are primordial essences unchanged from the beginning of time. They wrap the audience in a maternal embrace. Witnesses to this occasion stand transfixed, bathed in the intimacy of the moment.

* * * *

The observers sense the approach of a resolution when Purdie brings his improvisation to a close. They clap. The spell is broken, and chaos reigns once more. Purdie smiles and wipes the sweat from his face as he moves to the autograph table.

PART I
LEARNING TREE

1.

BUGSY

"Can I take you to the preacher? Let me take you to the preacher!" Bugsy shouts and waves his hands as he jumps into the path of the oncoming car he's spotted—one with New York tags. A young soldier in uniform pulls his new 1949 Ford coupe to the side of Route 40. After a brief conversation with the boy, he nods to his female passenger, who then lets Bugsy into the backseat. The car exits the highway with the youngster giving directions.

The soldier glances back at his young passenger. "You're going to get yourself killed out on this road. What's your name?"

"They call me Bugsy, sir," the boy says proudly. "Make a right up here."

Neat clapboard cottages with small porches appear behind the trees lining both sides of the street, as signs announcing the matrimonial services of several parsons in town vie for the soldier's attention.

LET THE DRUMS SPEAK!

Taxicabs had long ago monopolized the train-station and bus-stop wedding trade, so Bugsy worked the highway, where he could give directions from the backseat, expecting a generous tip from the happy groom at the end of the ride, in addition to a finder's fee from the parson.

"It's on the next block. The parson will take care of you," Bugsy says. He sounds confident as he brings his clients to a big corner house with four large signs on the front lawn, each with a different silhouette but all announcing the same message: "MINISTER-MARRIAGE-LICENSE." While the car is pulling up to the house, a matronly woman steps out onto the front porch. Bugsy waves to her from the backseat, then rushes ahead of the couple as they walk toward the porch steps.

Bugsy beams with his brightest smile as he bounces up the steps two at a time. "Hello, Mrs. Sears," he says to the wife of one of the ministers who performs wedding ceremonies.

"Hi, Bugsy," she says quickly, turning her attention to the couple now coming toward her. Bugsy moves to her side.

"You look lovely, dear," Mrs. Sears says to the young woman as the couple approaches. The bride looks up from beneath her bonnet and smiles.

"The parson is just completing a wedding ceremony. He won't be long. Come into the parlor and be comfortable while you wait. Let me get you something to drink," Mrs. Sears offers.

She does not wait for a reply and quickly returns carrying a silver tray with two tall glasses of iced tea, each with a stirrer and a sprig of mint. Mrs. Sears's gestures are carefully choreographed. She has done this many times.

Bugsy observes her through the screen door. His clients stand nervously in the parlor, and he can hear the parson's voice coming from beyond the room. Mrs. Sears feels his small presence at the front door and turns abruptly to go out to the porch. Bugsy steps back. She hands him fifty cents. "Thank you, Mrs. Sears," Bugsy says in response. He bounds down the porch stairs and sprints back to the highway.

Since the 1920s, Elkton, Maryland, has been known as the "Marriage Capital of the East." The State of Maryland does not have a waiting period for the issuance of marriage licenses. The first county seat one encounters when traveling into Maryland by road or rail from the populous northeast, Elkton has had little competition in attracting lovesick couples looking for quick, uncomplicated marriages. The city's motels run perpetual "Honeymoon Specials," and ready-to-wear wedding bands are prominently displayed in store windows along its Main Street. Taxi drivers pitch package deals that include transportation first to a parson, then to the honeymoon suite, and finally, back to the train station or bus depot, with a wedding band thrown in for good measure.

One Elkton minister reportedly performed more than 4,000 weddings in one year. Elkton's reputation as a wedding mill was so widespread that during the Second World War, the United States' military campaign against the Japanese on Rabaul, New Britain, was named "Operation Elkton" because it "married" the Army of General Douglas MacArthur with the Navy of Admiral William "Bull" Halsey. Ethel Merman, Bert Lahr, Joan Fontaine, Cornel Wilde, Billie Holliday, Willie Mays, and Screamin' Jay Hawkins are among the celebrities issued marriage licenses at the Cecil County Courthouse in Elkton.

As a child, Bugsy was taking his first tentative steps into the flow of America's cultural history.

BERNARD PURDIE

During the Great Depression, James and Mary Purdie moved from North Carolina and settled in Elkton. James found work on the track gang of the Pennsylvania Railroad and on the highway building crew for Route 40, a section of a cross-continental highway funded under President Franklin Roosevelt's New Deal. After the highway opened, James took a job as a cook at the Elkton Diner, which opened along the same road. Mary Purdie gave birth to sixteen children in as many years, but only nine of her children survived infancy: six sons in succession followed by three daughters. Dr. James Johnson, Cecil County's only black physician, delivered all of her children, including her fifth son, who arrived on June 11, 1942. James and Mary named him Bernard Lee Purdie. Henry, their oldest son, nicknamed him "Bugsy."

Mary Purdie was a big woman, standing nearly six feet four inches. She towered over James, who stood five feet eight. Mary lived for her children and her husband. Her world was her kitchen, where she prepared meals for her family on a coal-burning pot-bellied stove. Up before dawn, Mary started her day by boiling water for bathing (there were no indoor facilities). She would bake bread, prepare breakfast for the Purdie clan, and make lunches for the schoolchildren. During the day, Mary kept her infant child (there always was one) in an unadorned basket sitting on a kitchen chair, while a two-year-old scuttled around the kitchen floor. Each new arrival went into the basket, marking the graduation of the next oldest child to explore the kitchen; meanwhile, the next oldest moved on to a life of small household chores.

Despite his height, James was a very powerful man. It was said that he could carry an entire section of steel railroad track on his shoulder unaided. James earned reputations for working hard and fighting hard, and he was proud of both. His reputation for prowess with his fists was so widely known that out-of-town toughs would approach him in groups and challenge him to fight. If he couldn't talk them out of a fight, he would make sure he got close enough to throw the first punch. Staring menacingly into the leader's eyes, he never threatened, but if he sensed a punch was coming, he would hit the leader first as hard as he could, trying to hurt the man severely with one punch. That blow usually ended the fight. James Purdie never backed down from a fight, a conviction that he passed on to his sons.

Then there was the elderly Cap: a surrogate grandfather to the Purdie children and a calming influence on the fiery James. James never questioned Cap, no matter how agitated he might become. Cap needed only to place his hand on James's shoulder; James would stop and respond immediately with a respectful, "Yes, sir!" How Cap and James established their relationship is a mystery, but from the children's point of view, Cap had always been there. He was considered their grandfather, even though their paternal grandfather was alive and resided on the Purdie family farm outside of Elizabethtown, North Carolina.

Lying east of the Susquehanna Flats along the Big Elk Creek for which it is named, Elkton sits at the head of the Chesapeake Bay, one of the world's great estuaries. . The land on which Elkton is situated was once the property of Robert Alexander, a British sympathizer during the Revolutionary War who sailed back to England after the colonies won their independence.

After Alexander's departure, his property was confiscated and subdivided. The principal residence of Alexander's estate sits on the bank of Big Elk Creek, then the town's primary access to the Chesapeake Bay and the source of its early commerce. Subsequent owners named the Elkton estate "The Hermitage," after the Nashville, Tennessee, homestead of President Andrew Jackson. James Purdie was the caretaker of Elkton's Hermitage estate. James and his older sons kept the grounds and tended to the Hermitage residence and nearby apartment buildings owned by several merchant families with a financial interest in the estate. To the Purdie family, it was simply "the farm."

Shortly before Bernard's birth, World War II turned the sleepy village of Elkton into a boomtown. The population of Cecil County tripled almost overnight. The principal naval training center for the East Coast was opened only fifteen miles west in Bainbridge, Maryland. At its peak the Bainbridge Naval Training Center housed nearly 35,000 recruits on the 1,000-acre property, which became the site of hundreds of barracks, training halls, classrooms, gymnasiums, and mess halls. A small fireworks factory in Elkton was pressed into service making naval munitions. The United States government took over the facility, and 1,000 self-contained buildings were constructed on the site, located far enough apart so that, if one building exploded, it wouldn't take the whole town with it in a chain reaction.

Government recruiters traveled as far away as North Carolina and West Virginia to search for workers willing to move to Elkton to pack shells at minimum wage. The federal government recruited women and blacks for the tedious work. Approximately 50,000 job announcements were dropped from airplanes over the backwoods of West Virginia, and by 1943, more than 11,000 new workers had invaded Elkton. Another 6,000 people arrived in their wake. Off-hour crowds roamed the streets looking for entertainment in a town that was bursting at its seams.

Yet entertainment was in short supply in Elton. Philadelphia and Baltimore were too distant to provide an outlet for wartime employees and military personnel; to alleviate the situation, the newly formed United Services Organization (USO) established one of its first centers in Elton. While the USO provided some activities, these did not address the needs of war industry workers, particularly black workers.

These new arrivals found their way to local black clubs and dance halls in the county and provided a source of increased business for a local orchestra led by two Elton brothers, Clyde and Pete Bessicks. The Clyde Bessicks Orchestra played engagements from rural Maryland counties northeast of Baltimore to the Brandywine Valley of Pennsylvania and down the eastern shore of the bay into Delaware and Maryland. The orchestra consisted of fourteen instrumentalists and played the popular dance music of the day. Jazz arrangements made popular by Duke Ellington, Count Basie, and Benny Goodman were the orchestra's standard material. Clyde Bessicks, a local high school music teacher, insisted his orchestra also learn and rehearse the latest hit songs, and he made sure his musicians had written arrangements. It was a remarkable organization to emerge from a town the size of Elton. Clyde Bessicks was committed to playing at a high level, even if he was relegated to venues outside the larger cities. The orchestra's drummer was Leonard Heywood, another music teacher at George Washington Carver School in Elkton, the public school for colored students in Cecil County. In a few years, Heywood would take on a talented and relentlessly ambitious young apprentice.

At the age of two, Bugsy found himself with a fifth brother, Richard, nicknamed Hedgie. Hedgie bumped Bugsy from the kitchen basket to the kitchen floor, where Bugsy rode around on his mother's leg for a good part of the day. When he was old enough, Bugsy accompanied his father and older brothers as they went about their chores tending the property's grounds, making repairs, and cleaning the houses and apartments. They also planted and harvested crops on the several acres of land at the northern end of the property that lay between the Pennsylvania railroad tracks and Big Elk Creek.

Sometimes James would bring home food from the diner (though both James and Mary were excellent cooks), and the family ate well. Cap tended a vegetable garden, and the Purdie family raised chickens and other farm animals. James also raised hunting dogs. Cap sold medicinal ointments, cures, and remedies. He kept his apothecary in a salesman's case under his bed. Skilled in the distiller's art, Cap kept an inventory of his homemade wines and other spirits as well. As Cap was very popular, a steady stream of "visitors" went in and out of the Purdie home. One day young

Bugsy found his way into a bottle of homemade gin. It didn't take the family long to figure out why he was giggling and staggering around the house. When World War II ended, the thundering munitions testing on the western bank of the bay at the Aberdeen Proving Grounds ceased for a time. Elkton, like the rest of the country, started readjusting to peacetime. The naval munitions plant west of town closed, laying off 12,000 workers, and the massive Naval Training School in Port Deposit closed its doors as well. But a significant number of displaced workers stayed in the area, and by the end of the war, Elkton's population had doubled.

Bugsy was an outgoing child who had a gift. His fascination with percussion blossomed literally at his mother's knee, as he scuttled around on her kitchen floor, cobbling together a contraption of his own design from pots, pans, pie tins, and a commercial-sized potato chip container that his father brought home from the diner. Bugsy's mother had used the container to store bread, but she let her son incorporate it into his homemade drum set.

With the container serving as both a drum throne and a bass drum, Bugsy capped each knee with a pot or a pan or a pie tin and played a beat in his own fashion. He was fascinated with the contrast of sounds. He marveled at the bright sound of a small pie tin struck with a butter knife, weaving a bright rhythmic pattern through the darker sound of the bread can as he struck it with a wooden spoon.

LET THE DRUMS SPEAK!

Bugsy gradually broadened his percussion ensemble to include the hambone and added tap dancing to his rhythmic repertoire. Between the ages of three and six, he became quite accomplished. These were Bugsy's "bim-banging" beginnings.[1]

Bugsy drew his inspiration from everyday sounds. Alert to their patterns, he constantly turned them over in his mind. One Sunday morning, he noticed the lilt of a preacher calling to his flock. Bugsy observed that in the preacher's delivery of the sermon, he moved his congregation by using softly spoken phrases following a shout or a bellowed expression. The preacher got the congregation's attention with a thunderous exhortation and then fed them the message in a turn of phrase that he barely whispered.[2]

Each spring, James and Mary drove south with the younger children to the Purdie family farm in North Carolina. The farm stood near the banks of the Cape Fear River on the outskirts of Elizabethtown. The older of the children picked cotton, potatoes, tobacco, and other cash crops during the day. Since the harvest of each picker was weighed at the end of the day, the picking was quite competitive, even among the children. James's eleven brothers and sisters lived on the Purdie farm with their spouses and children. In the evenings after supper the adults would sit on their front porches to smoke and tell stories, while all family members would listen to the radio. Some evenings the adult conversation would turn to the subject of the Purdie family history. Bugsy was all ears.

According to the porch talk, the farm had been handed down from Bugsy's great-great-great grandfather, Henry James Purdie, who emigrated from Canada in the service of a Canadian landowner of Scottish descent named James Purdie. James Purdie had settled in the area at the beginning of the eighteenth century. The Purdie family inherited the land from James Purdie, who's will stipulated that if any of the other Purdie heirs challenged the bequest to Henry James Purdie, they would forfeit their own inheritances.

The surname Purdie—Scottish, but of French origin—is quite prominent around Elizabethtown. Highland Scots seeking refuge from religious oppression in their homeland first settled Bladen County, North Carolina, in the middle of the eighteenth century. Elizabethtown was a natural trading center, situated as it was, about fifty miles upstream from the seaport of Wilmington. It was eventually designated the county seat.

In 1786, one James S. Purdie served as both county sheriff and county clerk. In 1861, Thomas James Purdie joined the Confederate Army as a private in the Bladen Guards of the North Carolina Militia. He rose to the rank of colonel in the Army of Northern

LET THE DRUMS SPEAK!

Virginia under General Robert E. Lee. Colonel Purdie was a dedicated confederate soldier, but he had the dubious distinction of mistakenly ordering his men to fire on Stonewall Jackson during the Battle of Chancellorsville. Jackson died of his wounds three days later. Colonel Purdie was killed the next morning from a bullet to the head, reportedly fired from a Union sniper's rifle. The colonel's funeral was held at Purdie Methodist Church near Elizabethtown. For many years Colonel Purdie's uniform was on display at his birthplace, Purdie Hall, a mansion that sits on the banks of the Cape Fear River, a few miles north of Elizabethtown.

Henry Purdie's descendants built homes on the land and farmed it, raising tobacco, cotton, watermelon, peanuts, alfalfa, and corn. They kept hounds for hunting and horses for pulling and plowing. In general, children had free run of the farm as long as they did their chores. They could sleep over and have meals at a different house each day if they wished, and Bugsy often did. He worked in the fields, played with his cousins, and stuffed himself with the seemingly endless variety of food served each day. Occasionally, his father took him hunting. In the evenings, an attentive Bugsy listened, as the adults sat on their front porches smoking and spinning yarns. His inexhaustible curiosity produced an abundance of questions. At times, Bugsy would attempt to dominate the conversation until an adult finally invoked the rule that "children should be seen and not heard."

Not as much is known about Mary's family. Her mother, Mary Sheridan McNeil, had moved to Cecil County, Maryland, with her only son Robert Lee, before Mary. Mary's older sister, Ruth Estelle, was born in Robeson County, North Carolina, which is very near Elizabethtown. Another sister of Mary's became a schoolteacher in Chicago. It is believed that Mary's side of the family descended from Native Americans.

Twice a month the whole Purdie clan would pack food, leave the farm, and travel into Elizabethtown to join other local families for a customary Saturday picnic at the public park. It didn't take very long for someone to start playing a musical instrument—a guitar, harmonica, or a fiddle—and then dancing would ensue. At the first opportunity, little Bugsy would grab two metal spoons and play them like castanets while he chanted in rhythm with a feeling that seemed uniquely his own. He beamed with joy as the dancers responded in tempo and added their own flourishes to the flow of sounds that seemed to emanate from the very soul of the little boy.

In Elkton, the Purdie family lived in a two-bedroom house on Milburn Street. The attic was converted into bedroom space as more children arrived. The older children were responsible for taking care of the younger ones. Ernie looked out for Bugsy, and Bugsy took care of Hedgie—right on down the line. All the Purdie children were about two years apart in age. The pecking order was Henry-Nate-Tommy-Ernie-Bernard-Richard-Dolores-Betty-Thelma. The boys slept three to a bed in one room, and the girls had a different room for themselves, which doubled as a guest room.

The black section of Elkton was like an extended family. People in the neighborhood were connected in ways that made its boundaries more than merely a residential area; it was a functional village within the town itself. Bugsy made friends readily. The Sewell brothers—George, Norman, and Charlie—lived next door, with Norman being Bugsy's best friend. Across the street lived Rayfield Hammond and Clifford Jones. Norman Sewell was Bugsy's best friend. Mrs. Addie lived up the street and sold dinners from her house every Friday and Saturday evening for two dollars and fifty cents a plate: fried fish and fried chicken with generous portions of collard and mustard greens, corn bread, black-eyed peas, and potato salad, or, if you preferred, macaroni salad or rice. Mrs. Addie sold her own hooch by the half pint, and on occasion Cap's distinctive vintage would find its way into her stock. On Friday and Saturday evenings Mrs. Addie's front door was swinging harder than a New York jam session, with people coming and going, balancing plates piled high with homemade soul food. Just around the corner lived Clyde Bessicks (the orchestra leader and a music teacher at George Washington Carver School) and his wife, Thelma, (a first-grade teacher). A few steps away lived Clyde's brother Pete Bessicks. Dr. James Johnson lived in the next block, near Mrs. Fitzgerald, the history teacher. Even mailman Fred was adopted as part of the neighborhood family, because he always had a word of encouragement for folks, especially for little Bugsy.

At the age of five, Bugsy began to venture beyond his mother's kitchen, past Cap's garden, and out into the world of his neighborhood. One day, as he explored his new world and tested the limits of his emancipation from his mother's kitchen, he became aware of the sound of drums—and he followed that sound.

It led him down the block and as far as the corner because this was as far as he was permitted to go. He couldn't tell from which house the drumbeat came, but it sounded like it was across the street and up the next block over, on Bells Lane. Bugsy was on a mission. He had to get to that house. So, he went to Ernie. Would Ernie take him across the street and up that street? He would indeed. Ernie took him across High Street and up Bells Lane to a white house with a picture window, the home of Mr. Leonard Heywood. The front door was open. Bugsy approached the house and sat on the porch steps, listening to drums playing inside. Ernie told Bugsy to wait there until he came back to take him home. After an hour, Ernie returned to find Bugsy sitting in the same spot listening intently. Bugsy hadn't moved.

Soon Mr. Heywood noticed that he had a little visitor on his stoop whenever he was giving drum lessons. Mr. Heywood was a serious musician and a stern disciplinarian. He warned the little boy that he didn't want him to interfere with his lessons. Bugsy understood. He could be "seen but not heard." Bugsy was happy just to be there. And so he learned Mr. Heywood's teaching schedule and sat quietly on the stoop whenever Mr. Heywood was giving lessons. When the lessons were over, Bugsy would return home and practice what he had heard on his own makeshift kitchen drum set until his mother chased him out of her kitchen. As mouthy as Bugsy could be at other times, he was a model of decorum on Mr. Heywood's stoop.

As Bugsy grew older, he didn't need an escort to Bells Lane—but he also had more chores and responsibilities as he moved up in the Purdie pecking order. Henry enlisted in the Army, and Nate quickly followed him. Tommy would soon be leaving home as well. James Henry depended on Bugsy more and more to shoulder the load of the caretaking work at the farm and to help at the diner. With Thelma now in the kitchen basket and Delores and Betty helping Mary in the kitchen, Bugsy was on his own to deal with the world as a little man, and he was soon to start school.

The day started early in the Purdie household. Mary rose in the dark and prepared breakfast, while James and the boys washed up and tended to the morning chores. They all ate breakfast at a large table in the room off the kitchen, which served as both a living room and a dining hall. Henry, Nate, and Tommy would head off together to the George Washington Carver School, a short walk from the five-square-block neighborhood of black families where the Purdies lived. Ernie was usually left behind to take his two younger brothers to school.

From Bugsy's first day in school, he was in trouble. He expressed a know-it-all attitude with his teachers. His hand was always up at an age when most of his classmates were timid and shy. He argued with his teachers if he felt that he was getting inconsistent answers to his many questions. Some teachers loaded him down with work to keep him out of their hair. Others simply sent him to the principal's office. One of Bugsy's teachers discovered that Bugsy's memory was almost photographic. But all of his teachers readily discerned that he also had a super-sized ego. Bugsy couldn't understand why his classmates seemed to struggle over what came so easily to him. He was impatient to get on with things. He had places to go and people to see. There was no time to waste. This was long before the era when gifted children were put in special classes to be taught at an accelerated pace. Bugsy proved to be a problem, and most of his teachers didn't know what to do with him.

Space was at a premium in the Purdie house, as Mary continued to bear more children. Dr. Johnson had advised her to stop having children, but his advice went unheeded. In mock exaggeration, he is purported to have said, "Well, if James keeps putting them in there, I guess I'll have to keep taking them out." The difficulty of living in a family of twelve people crammed into what was essentially a two-bedroom house put a strain on the entire family. Cap had his own room, although some of the younger children would sneak into his room to sleep. James and Mary had their own room, and the infant child undoubtedly slept near Mary. That left six rambunctious boys and at least two of the three girls to live in two attic bedrooms.

At one point, James had an opportunity to move into a four-bedroom house on the Hermitage estate, where he worked as the caretaker. So, when Bugsy was eight, the family moved from the house on Milburn Street to the farm a quarter mile away. It was like heaven. The home had a cellar and four bedrooms, in addition to acres of land for gardening and playing. Big Elk Creek, where the children could fish, swim, or just romp around, bordered the property on the east. There was space to raise farm animals and hunting dogs. It was the answer to a prayer.

James and the boys maintained the apartments on the property, tended the grounds, and grew small stands of corn and other crops for market. Cap expanded his vegetable garden and stepped up his production of spirits to take advantage of the storage space in the cellar. Bugsy was now old enough to make the trip to Mr. Heywood's house on his own. But, in particular, this was a time of high spirits and great fun. All the Purdie boys were living at home, and they practically had enough players to field a full baseball lineup. It was the Purdie brothers against all challengers, with Betty, Dolores, and Thelma cheering them on. The release from cramped quarters was liberating, and family morale was high. The work was still exhausting and the hours long, but it seemed that the Purdie family was seeing better days after enduring many difficult years.

Each Purdie child was assigned chores from an early age. The children's tasks began with housework, and as they grew, they were assigned farm duties. The boys were indoctrinated into the caretaker's routine and the cleaning and maintenance of the apartments. Bugsy was no exception. He helped his mother in the house and worked in the garden with Cap. He helped Cap with his wine making and the distilling of spirits. His mother taught him to cook. When he grew older, he worked with his father and older brothers in the apartments and on the estate and helped at the Elkton Diner, where his father cooked an assortment of stews and other dishes in big navy pots. All the boys took their turns working at the diner. Tommy Purdie remembers:

"All my brothers—Ernie, Henry, Nate—all of us worked out there. I'll never forget it; they asked me what kind of work I do. I said, 'I majored in dishes and minored in pots and pans.' That's what it was because I had dishpan hands. I had calluses and corns when I used to work hard, but, you know, I don't have to work hard no more."

Even Mary helped out at the diner occasionally, whenever her mother was able to watch the babies; but the need to care for her young children kept her at home most of the time.

Bugsy, who inherited his father's great appetite for work, would brag about his father constantly: "My father works three jobs," he would boast. When Bugsy reached school age, he began to venture out into Elkton, canvassing downtown stores and offices for opportunities to run errands. With Hedgie in tow, he would visit Sheriff Nathan "Juicy" Kaplan at the county jail, then go to the firehouse and see Fire Chief Jack Jamison and Jamison's buddy, big rig truck driver Fletch Simmons, affectionately called "Uncle Fletch."

"One day they come walking down the street, neither one of them had shoes on. They couldn't even afford shoes. So, I took them down to the shoe store and bought them each a new pair of sneakers for $2 a pair. They weren't really that bad, just mischievous kids, and we never had any major problems." – Jack Jamison

Bugsy persisted in looking for work—any work. He constantly hustled, both out of poverty and for the sheer joy of it. He loved the money, and he loved the attention, too. Running errands for local merchants, delivering advertising flyers, and escorting couples to the preacher on weekends, Bugsy seemed to be everywhere in downtown Elkton all the time. A quarter here, fifty cents there; it all added up. He always had money. He turned most of it over to Cap, but he spent some, too. As Bugsy grew older, he loved to go out in the evenings and buy two containers of ice cream, a big bottle of orange soda pop, and a hefty tuna fish salad sandwich. He would come home, and when his younger siblings would beg him for food,

LET THE DRUMS SPEAK!

he'd fend them off with one of the containers of ice cream while he devoured the sandwich, drank the soda, and capped off his feast with the second container of ice cream.

"Bernard was a trip. He would come in like after he got all of his work done and everything, he'd come in with this ice cream, and he would make us do things for us to get some of the ice cream. That's what I remember of Bernard. He liked torturing us. We had to do this and do that to get some ice cream. It's like a torture to me. Yeah, I remember that most of all about him. I mean he did us all that way. And when he left, Hedgie took over doing the same thing Bernard used to do to us girls." – Dolores, Betty, and Thelma Purdie

One of his early jobs was shining shoes at a downtown shoe repair shop on Saturday afternoons. It wasn't long before Bugsy attracted an upscale clientele, who congregated at the shop while he displayed his rhythm magic with a shoeshine rag. The county judge, Sheriff Kaplan, Mayor John Stanley, Dr. James Johnson, and State Assemblyman William Burkley were all Bugsy's good customers. Bugsy didn't just shine shoes; he put on a show featuring his own choreographed shoeshine routine. The rag jumped and popped in an infectious rhythm that kept smiles on the faces of his customers and pulled big tips from their pockets. Soon his customers would come in for a shine only when they knew Bugsy was on the job.

Clearly, Bugsy's unique world, dominated by drumming, working odd jobs, and going to school, had begun to take shape. Bugsy admired his father, being particularly proud of James's work ethic. James Purdie was a man always in motion. He was either working on the railroad, working at the Elkton Diner, or working as a caretaker of the estate. He was not one to lounge about. Bugsy emulated James in that respect. He hustled odd jobs downtown, and he hustled the marriage trade on Saturday mornings. He shined shoes, collected bottles for deposits, and helped his father at the diner.

Bugsy was gaining a bit of prominence in Elkton. Gradually, his persistence with Mr. Heywood started to bear fruit. One day Mr. Heywood asked Bugsy to show him what he could do. Bugsy approached Mr. Heywood's drum set cautiously, mounted the drum throne, and began to play. Bugsy played his bim-bang beginnings, his kitchen rhythms, and his Elizabethtown beats. Finally, he played Mr. Heywood's lessons back to him. If Mr. Heywood had any doubts about Bugsy's musical potential, they were erased that day. But Heywood knew too well that it takes more than sheer talent to succeed as a musician. There are many pitfalls for a musician to whom the technical side of playing an instrument comes too easily. Musicianship is much more than just technique. It demands an attitude of humility in the face of great natural gifts, and at the same time it demands the confidence to do what is necessary to make the music come alive. Bugsy had the gift of talent and great confidence, but he needed to learn humility. So, Mr. Heywood set about training Bugsy's musical attitude. Bugsy became more than Mr. Heywood's student. He became his musical apprentice. Mr. Heywood let Bugsy sit on his living room steps during his lessons and occasionally would ask Bugsy to demonstrate a routine for one of his paying students, but he forbade the boy to speak during the lessons. Soon Mr. Heywood allowed Bugsy to come to his home to practice on the drum set, so Bugsy learned by observing and then practicing what he observed on his own. And when Bugsy was old enough, Mr. Heywood took him on engagements with the Clyde Bessicks Orchestra as a band boy.

As his apprentice, Bugsy would break down Mr. Heywood's drums and stow them in his station wagon, and off the two of them would go. One event that Bugsy particularly enjoyed was Elkton's concert in the town park. Held in the summer, it was a time for the whole town to enjoy good music, good barbecue, and dancing. The event was loosely segregated. Whites picnicked and danced on one side of the bandstand and blacks on the other; a section of chairs for all senior citizens sat directly in front of the bandstand. The event gave Bugsy an opportunity to play in front of the whole town because Mr. Heywood always let him play on at least one number.

Most of the orchestra's engagements were dances. It was at these engagements that Bugsy experienced his first taste of live adult musical entertainment. Sometimes the orchestra opened for one of the national bands traveling through Cecil County on the "Chitlin' Circuit." Of course, Bugsy would later extend his roadie responsibilities to include setting up for Sonny Greer, when Duke Ellington was on the bill, or for Jo Jones, when Count Basie was the draw. Because of his age, young Purdie was adopted as the gig mascot and would be given a chance to play. The next time the band came through, band members would remember Bugsy, which contributed to his ever-growing confidence and inflated ego. On other engagements, Bugsy would get valuable playing time when Mr. Heywood would pass out drunk in the station wagon during intermission: Bugsy would merely appear on the drum throne at the beginning of the next set and play out the rest of the night.

Bugsy emanated excitement at these dances. From the hardscrabble world he inhabited in Elkton, Bugsy entered a more elegant setting of suits, dresses, perfume, and cologne—of men and women dressed in their finest clothes, dancing to the incredibly sweet sounds from the bandstand. Bugsy was enchanted by the laughter floating above the buzz of animated conversation and thrilled at the hot numbers when the really good dancers would show off their latest moves. Young Bugsy took it all in and dreamed of a life for himself that would be quite different from the one he was living. He sat behind the stage with his eyes wide open, taking in the whole scene and dreaming the dream of a child awakened to the larger possibilities that the world outside Elkton had to offer. He wanted it.

Bugsy's musical talent was a source of pride to the whole family, and their residence on the Hermitage estate, even as caretakers, gave the Purdie family a higher profile. But as Bugsy's confidence grew, so did his pride. He was a quick study, and he knew he had a special gift for music. Mr. Heywood did what he could to keep Bugsy's ego reined in. One day, in his enthusiasm, Bugsy blurted out a comment during one of Mr. Heywood's lessons. Heywood ordered Bugsy to leave immediately. Bugsy left in tears. But he would not stay away. He pleaded with Mr. Heywood to take him back. Bugsy ran errands for Mr. Heywood's wife and pleaded with her to speak to her husband on his behalf. Mr. Heywood let Bugsy worry for a couple of days and then took him back.

Bugsy got his share of beatings at the hands of his father, but they might have saved his life. Bugsy discovered that, in addition to music and money, he loved something else: alcohol. At the age of eight, he started going to the liquor store in Elkton and giving the local winos money to buy liquor for him, usually a sweet, syrupy, orange mixed drink. As a matter of liquor store etiquette, the fronting wino got the first pull on the uncapped bottle. Bugsy hated this unsanitary ritual, so he would wipe the mouth of the bottle as clean as he could, and then pour the liquor down his throat without his lips touching the mouth of the bottle. When James suspected Bugsy of drinking, he beat him mercilessly. He wore poor Bugsy out. James was able to slow down Bugsy's drinking, though he wouldn't give up the bottle entirely.

James Purdie could be harsh, but his children still loved and admired him. He felt the need to prove himself the better man every week of his life. There was always someone challenging him to fight, and the more often he won the fights, the more often men came to challenge him. Purdie was the baddest, strongest man in Elkton and perhaps in all of Cecil County. He would fight and drink on the weekends, go to church on Sunday, and be at work sober and on time every Monday morning. Many men admired him for his seemingly limitless capacity for work and his fighting prowess. But there were those who saw him as a dangerous man who would come to a violent end.

Life on the farm seemed too good to last, and it didn't. Being illiterate, James had marked the contract with an "X. He had understood that the arrangement with the owners of the estate was to allow him to work off the mortgage on his house. The owners disagreed, and the dispute went to court. James lost the argument. So when Bugsy was eleven, his family moved back to the neighborhood and back to cramped quarters. Shortly after the move, Mary Purdie died.

Through Bugsy's young eyes, it seemed that one day in the summer of 1953, his mother could no longer cross the threshold of her own home. She would approach the door and then fall backward. Nor could she climb the stairs. So, a bed was set up in the living room. There she stayed, bedridden and steadily losing weight. One day, Cap took Bugsy for a ride in the direction of Baltimore. They drove for some distance before stopping at neat house surrounded by a white fence. Bugsy followed Cap through the fence gate, into the yard, and toward the front porch. A woman mysteriously appeared at the door, looked at Cap, and said, "You're too late. If you'd come a few days sooner . . . Place this package beneath the third step of the house, and she will be released from her misery." Cap took the package and left. Cap told Bugsy that his mother was under a spell of a neighborhood woman who was a rival for his father's affections.

Mary Purdie died a few days later. All Bugsy saw was the unoccupied bed in the living room. When he asked where his mother was, he was told she had passed. But as the family gathered in the living room around the empty bed, Bugsy started asking about the church picnic to Atlantic City the next day. His older siblings looked puzzled and said to him "But Mom is dead." Bugsy replied with great confidence, "I know she's dead. She'll be back." The older members of the family merely shook their heads sadly and said, "Let him go." The next morning, Bugsy, Hedgie, Thelma, Dolores, and Betty went to the picnic, which turned out to be the best day of Bugsy's young life. All the other church members fed him and his brother and sisters during the entire trip and treated them to all the rides. When they returned home, Bugsy curled up in the living room chair next to the empty mattress where his mother had died and fell into a peaceful sleep, confident of her return.

2.

RHYTHM PLANET

"Rooted deep in physiological grounds as functions of our bodies, rhythm permeates melody, form, and harmony; it becomes the driving and shaping force, indeed, the very breath of music, and reaches up into the loftiest reaches of aesthetic experience, where description is doomed to fail because no language provides the vocabulary for adequate words."
– Curt Sachs, <u>Rhythm and Tempo</u>
W.W. Norton & Company, NY (1953)

The end of the Second World War marked the end of the Jazz Age. Big bands were dying. There was bebop, but bebop wasn't dance music, and without the patronage of the dance audience, the new jazz music did not inherit the commercial success enjoyed by the big jazz bands of the twenties, thirties, and forties. Moreover, the country needed a new kind of anthem. Americans wanted to celebrate in the style of a people who had delivered the world from the brutal grip of fascism. They longed to put aside the grim spirit of determination necessary to overcome the Great Depression and to win the Second World War. Rhythm and blues and its progeny, rock 'n' roll, would provide that "new spirit" in musical forms that leaned heavily upon the central feature of African music, percussive rhythm.

It's ironic that the drum—the one musical instrument so feared in the hands of African slaves that it was a crime for a slave to possess one—would become the centerpiece of American popular music. The spirit of the drum adheres to the rhythm of the person who plays it. In the Western mind, the spirit of African rhythm is the spirit of primitive man—unsophisticated, violent, wild, rebellious, all facets of the image associated with the "dark heart" of the African continent. One war had ended, but another—a cultural one—was heating up.

One of Bugsy's musical heroes was Earl Palmer. Earl Palmer was drafted into the United States Army during World War II and sent to Europe to fight the Germans, but Palmer was so fiercely independent that he was constantly under threat of a court-martial. Before the war, he had been a child dancer alongside his mother and his auntin a black vaudeville troupe. He intended to continue his dancing career after the war.

Palmer managed to be honorably discharged and returned home to New Orleans to find a still-vibrant music scene, but vaudeville had died. He discovered that he had a natural affinity for the drums, so he began playing around town. As he became more involved in his instrument, he used his GI benefits to study musical composition. Soon he was one of the most sought-after jazz drummers in New Orleans.

After the war, record companies began looking for the next big thing in music. In New Orleans, they found a shy singer/piano player calling himself Fats Domino. They also found an outrageous singer/piano player going by the name of Little Richard. In the backroom studio of Cosimo Matassa's J&M Music at Rampart and Dumaine Streets—a store that also sold records, radios, televisions, washing machines, and refrigerators—a band to accompany these early prospects in recording sessions was organized.

Palmer got the call to play drums in these sessions. The music didn't really appeal to him, but as the sessions went on, he began to hear the music he was playing to a little differently. His sensibility to the subtle flow of the jazz idiom gave birth to a defining rhythmic emphasis. Palmer transformed the triplet feel of jazz into the backbeat. The seeds planted earlier by bandleader Louis Jordan had flowered. "Race music" became "rhythm and blues," "hillbilly" tunes were now termed "country and western" music, and, in a defiant act of musical miscegenation, a country and western singer named Bill Haley recorded a composition titled "Rock Around the Clock." The Rock and Roll era had begun.

Bugsy loved it all. His love affair with music was maturing into an appreciation for musical styles. He was discovering his own musical tastes. He loved country and western music. Mr. Heywood reinforced Bugsy's appreciation for country music by displaying a gift for playing it on his accordion. In the popular vein, Teresa Brewer's "Nickelodeon" and Cozy Cole's "Topsy" were Bugsy's favorites.

Bugsy had learned most of the Clyde Bessicks Orchestra arrangements, and he was able to keep up with new material. He was becoming an increasingly proficient reader, and he was getting more playing time as Mr. Heywood seemed to retire to the backseat of his station wagon earlier and earlier with each passing engagement. Musically, he advanced very quickly.

Mr. Heywood knew Bugsy could handle first chair in the high school orchestra though still attending elementary school, so he switched him to trumpet and flute to avoid embarrassing the older students and to give Bugsy more familiarity with music's harmonic structure. Mr. Heywood also gave Bugsy an autoharp to help him learn harmony.

LET THE DRUMS SPEAK!

The orchestra was Bugsy's primary means of musical expression. He now got playing time equal to Mr. Heywood's. As a dance band, the orchestra continually introduced new material that was currently popular, so Bugsy was constantly being exposed to new written arrangements. These arrangements and Mr. Heywood's extensive collection of jazz recordings were Bugsy's early inspiration.

Bugsy also played in a neighborhood club called Burke's Tavern, popularly known as "The Field." Mr. Heywood and other members of the orchestra jammed at The Field as well, but Bugsy would always hustle Mr. Heywood's drum set into the club early and get things started long before Mr. Heywood had even left home. This gave young Bugsy a commanding situation with other musicians, since there was only one drum set, and Bugsy controlled it, at least until Mr. Heywood arrived. Bugsy's father, his older brothers, and Cap frequented The Field." While still a boy, Bugsy was keeping adult company with the adult members of his own family in an adult setting.

Bugsy was proud of his abilities on the drums and the recognition it brought him. He began to develop an act in which he would sing and generally entertain from the drum throne. Occasionally, other musicians would sit in on drums. One afternoon, after Bugsy had just played a drum solo in a flamboyant style, a white youngster

Bugsy's own age approached him on the bandstand and asked to play.

When the boy took the drum throne, he looked up at Bugsy and said, "Now this is how you played that solo." Then, in front of the whole club, he proceeded to cut Bugsy mercilessly, playing Bugsy's own solo stroke for stroke but more precisely and prettier than Bugsy had played it. After he'd played the solo, he told Bugsy, "This is how you should have played it." The boy then proceeded to play a solo that to Bugsy's mind was ten times better than what he had played. Bugsy was shocked, embarrassed, and humiliated. The boy left the club. Bugsy never saw him again. But a resolve hardened in Bugsy's mind that never left him. He would never be caught unprepared again. There might be other drummers with better technique than he, but no drummer would play prettier than he played. That afternoon gave birth to an obsession that would drive him throughout his extraordinary professional career: Bugsy would embody a musical ideal that would become known in the person of Bernard "Pretty" Purdie.

* * * *

Adjusting to Mary's death was difficult for the Purdie family. There were three young girls and no women in the Purdie home. Mary's mother lived ten miles away, in Cecilton, and she stayed in Elkton for short periods of time to help run the household, a responsibility that seemed to rest more and more on the shoulder of old Cap, who was now over ninety years old.

"Mom's girlfriend was Maggie Byrd. I'll never forget her. She came down to the house—the girls had just been born—and told them, 'Look, don't worry about nothing. I'll take care and make sure that the women see that everything is done for the girls.' And we really had help from the people that she knew. There were two of them. I remember Mrs. Maggie Byrd was one of them. It's amazing how they came up. Cap was at the house. He was like mother and father. Daddy would get up and sunup to sundown, one job to another. But we were just fortunate that a lot of ladies came in and took care of the girls, because we didn't know [how]. They had baths and all like that, but far as everything else about girls, we didn't know about it. And they wanted to try to take the girls away because there was no woman in the house. Mrs. Byrd said, 'No, no, no! I'll make sure that the girls are taken care of.' That was one of the things that kept them from taking the girls. They figured the boys could make it but with the three girls there—she made sure that that didn't happen." – Henry Purdie

After the death of his mother Bugsy had his hands full. Even though Cap was at home and Bugsy's Grandmother Mary frequently came to help out, the Purdie children had to shoulder more responsibility around the house. Between school, house chores, hustling the marriage trade, odd jobs, keeping up with new orchestra arrangements, practice, performances, and efforts to form his own band on the side, Bugsy was constantly in motion. Money was always tight, but Bugsy had his eye on a better job that would give him a steadier source of income.

In 1919 A. F. Stanley ran a newsstand located in the old Howard Hotel on Main Street. When the hotel burned down in 1927, Stanley moved it across the street to a building once used to store grain for troops during the Revolutionary War. Eventually A.F.'s son, John Stanley, took over his father's business.

John Stanley had an interest in politics, so in 1963 he ran for mayor of Elkton and won. He served as Elkton's mayor for sixteen years. Bugsy, in his canvass of Main Street for work, ran errands for Stanley, such as passing out flyers. But Bugsy wanted a steadier source of income—delivering newspapers—and Stanley was the man to see. Bugsy pestered Stanley, but he couldn't seem to work his way into the job. Then suddenly one of Stanley's paperboys quit, and Bugsy, who always kept his ears open for any news as important as that, was right in Stanley's store, pleading for a chance to do the job. Stanley gave it to him.

On his bicycle, Bugsy delivered the <u>Cecil Whig</u>, the <u>Cecil Democrat</u>, the <u>Baltimore Sun</u>, the <u>Wilmington News Journal</u>, the <u>Philadelphia Inquirer</u>, and the <u>Afro-American</u> from Baltimore. On Sundays, however, he would deliver the big Sunday editions with Stanley in his van. If anyone in Elkton didn't know Bernard "Bugsy" Purdie from his sojourns downtown, they would certainly know him now: little Bugsy who worked for John Stanley, the mayor of Elkton.

The news that summer had been of particular interest to Bugsy's neighborhood. The United States Supreme Court announced that racial segregation of the nation's public schools was unconstitutional. The decision resulted from the <u>Brown v. Board of Education</u> case. One of the cases in the decision was from Delaware, whose border was a mere five miles from downtown Elkton. The Wilmington, Delaware, paper that Bugsy delivered covered the effect of the decision almost daily, as the Delaware State Board of Education had ordered Delaware school boards to implement desegregation plans for the upcoming 1954–1955 school year. The State of Maryland was reviewing the decision to determine what action it would take. At the time, Bugsy was only going to enter the seventh grade at George Washington Carver School, but he was definitely interested in eventually attending

Elkton High School. He was watchful for what the State of Maryland would do.

Meanwhile Bugsy's work with Stanley steadily grew. He took over more paper routes and worked at the newsstand on Main Street, stocking shelves and helping customers. He got up every Sunday at 3:30 a.m. to meet the news delivery trucks at the newsstand. He spent the next several hours stuffing the sections of the big Sunday editions of the <u>Baltimore Sun</u>, the <u>Philadelphia Inquirer</u>, the <u>New York Times</u>, and the <u>Wilmington News Journal</u>.

Mayor Stanley would meet him at the newsstand with his van, and together they delivered the Sunday papers all over Elkton. Stanley even let Bugsy drive his van, although he was too young to drive legally. But the police never stopped Bugsy for driving Stanley's van, even if Stanley wasn't with him. The state police, the Elkton police, and the county sheriff all knew that Bugsy worked for the mayor. Bugsy began to realize that his association with Stanley brought him certain extraordinary privileges.

The people of Elkton began to associate Bugsy with Stanley and tried to pump Bugsy for information of interest to them. Bugsy loved to talk, but he knew well enough to keep Stanley's confidences. Stanley trusted him, and Bugsy was old enough to realize what that meant. Because he was the mayor, Stanley would be drawn into conversations all along the Sunday route, so he'd send Bugsy ahead alone in the truck to keep the deliveries on schedule and then catch up with the van on foot. Bugsy hated to be slowed down like that. He wanted to finish and get home, but he began to get a glimpse of what it meant to be mayor.

After the work was done, Stanley would take Bugsy with him for breakfast at a local restaurant. There, Bugsy could sit and eat in total defiance of the customary Jim Crow restrictions. At breakfast Mr. Stanley would at times hold some serious discussion with another political official over town business. Bugsy was right there, taking it all in. This was a whole different world from the one he knew, and he was privy to it. It made him feel special and destined to stand apart from the crowd. Certainly, no one else his own age whom he knew was having these experiences.

As Bugsy approached his thirteenth birthday, he continued to drink, but James was wearing him down. He began to beat Bugsy whether Bugsy was drinking or not. Bugsy was getting tired of being beaten almost every day, so he finally gave up the bottle and never went back to it.

Proud of all his children, James tried to help them as much as he could in his own way. Now that Bugsy had stopped drinking, he now felt that it was time for Bugsy to have his own drums. Money was tight, but somehow James was determined to buy Bugsy a set of drums for Christmas that year.

James wasn't a flagrant spender. He was in the habit of turning his pay over to Mary, who would in turn give him an allowance. The family was smaller now, but after the lawsuit, James was no longer the caretaker of the Hermitage, and he was now paying rent on Collins Avenue. After work on the Friday evening before Christmas of 1955, James took his pay to Hickman's Sawmill on Old North East Road near Beacon Hill, Maryland, and there he shot craps with his friend Pete Baker, the night watchman. Baker had visited the Purdie home often enough that the Purdie children called him Uncle Pete. The game went on late into the night and early into the Saturday morning of Christmas Eve. Purdie remembers,

"Yeah. He had won all this money, about $400 he had won, so he asked [Uncle Pete] to take him home, you know; of course, that was fine, [since] it was six miles away. Then, when he got home, he asked [my father] for $2, and my father said no, he was taking all that money home and was going to give it to the kids and let them have a good Christmas. And the man said that if you don't, I'll blow your head off. My father went and turned the car around, and Uncle Pete went inside and got the shotgun. He came out and said, 'See,

told you I'll blow your head off if you don't give me that $2.' And my father knocked the gun up, the gun went off, right here, hit him in the chest, and my father drove six miles to the house, went right past the hospital, tried to get to the house, and then he slumped over the wheel one block from the house. Georgie Porgie, who's our friend, saw him and came running down and got us. Then we took him to the hospital. He died the second day after Christmas 'cause he had lost so much blood and they couldn't get enough into him fast enough. Uncle Pete was Daddy's best friend, and after Daddy died, well, two men died that day."

Hedgie also remembers that awful time.

"I can remember him coming home, driving home from wherever he got shot. I saw a hole in his chest about the size of a saucer. When I went, he was in the car in the driver's seat in front of the house. He had driven home several miles from wherever he was shot. One of my brothers, they took him down to the hospital. And he lived for four or five days—about four or five days he lived. And at that time we asked the preacher man, Oral Roberts, for prayer and healing and so forth. Then I could remember making promises that I'd be a good boy, and when he did pass, I was upset. I think the whole family was upset, but I told God I didn't like him for not doing what I asked him to do because I was going to be good. Bernard handled it pretty tough. Henry handled it the worst. At the *funeral he ran from the church down to the jail to kill the man, but they caught him and stopped him."*

James's violent death put into question again the future of the Purdie family. The only adult in the household now was Cap. Cap wasn't legally related to the Purdies, and he was approaching one hundred years of age. After the funeral, a social worker began visiting the Purdie home, again renewing the prospect that the children might be placed in foster homes. Bugsy noticed that although his Grandmother Mary lived in Cecilton, she was always at their house when the social worker showed up on Collins Avenue. His grandmother's timing was uncanny. Purdie recalls,

"I know that one time the lady showed up, and it was like saying, 'Ah-ha!' and we were just looking at her, and they wanted to know, you know, where our grandmom was. I said, 'Well, she must be out to the store.' Five minutes later, grandmom would come there with groceries."

With the loss of James's income, the Purdie family was hard-pressed to survive. The older boys and even the younger children contributed as they were able. Occasionally, Bugsy would make a little extra money playing music. He had a few isolated engagements, but since he was limited to borrowing Mr.

Heywood's drums, he couldn't take on more paying gigs even if they were offered.

One engagement he really looked forward to was Ringling Bros. Barnum and Bailey Circus. The circus came to Cecil County every summer. Typically, the circus band would augment its personnel with local musicians, and Mr. Heywood arranged for Bugsy to play during its stay. For Bugsy this was heaven. The arrangements were theatrical, and you had to watch for the cues, but playing with the circus was a blast—and he got paid. There was no question in Bugsy's mind that he wanted to be a professional musician, but for now music wouldn't pay the bills.

* * * *

After James's death, John Stanley virtually adopted Bugsy. Although Bugsy still shined shoes and worked the marriage trade, his paper routes became his primary source of income. He saw John Stanley every day, and on Sundays they worked side by side. Mayor Stanley's daughter remembers her father and Bugsy making their routine Sunday morning pit stop at the Stanley home. Stanley would head for the bathroom, and Bugsy would head for the pantry. Their closeness was so obvious that people referred to Bugsy as the mayor's son. Perhaps it was Bugsy's energy or his talent or his personality, or a combination of all three, that the mayor liked about him. Perhaps it was the loss of his mother and father that drew

Bugsy closer to Stanley, but the two could not have been closer if they had been father and son.

Stanley knew about Mary and James, the loss of the house on the farm, and the family's constant struggle against poverty and foster care. The Purdie family saga had unfolded over the years in Elkton, and Stanley was sympathetic. Knowing that something needed to be done for Bugsy and his family, he did it: he bought Bugsy a set of drums. Bugsy would be able to pay for it out of his paper route money, but he could have the drums immediately. Bugsy was ecstatic. He went to the local music store and purchased the most garish-looking drum kit he could find—a Rogers Scotch Plaid set. Stanley's gesture was a vote of confidence in him, and it kept Bugsy focused on his future and on his love of music. Music and the life lessons he had learned from Cap, his mother, his father, Mr. Heywood, Mayor Stanley, and the town of Elkton had sustained him. He had no doubt now that he and his family would be all right.

But shortly after James's death, Mr. Heywood told Bugsy he was moving to Arizona to help treat his respiratory ailment. Suddenly Mr. Heywood was out of Bugsy's life as well, and although Bugsy later received several letters from him, he never saw Mr. Heywood again. Mr. Heywood and the Clyde Bessicks Orchestra had been a big part of Bugsy's life. He hoped that Mr. Bessicks would offer him Heywood's drum chair. Bugsy knew the musical arrangements, and now he had his own drum set. Hadn't he driven that big band in the second half of the night when Mr. Heywood inevitably went into his cups? But, for whatever reason, now that Mr. Heywood was out of the band, Bugsy was also out. He played pick up sets here and there, but nothing like his work with the orchestra. He tried to pull his own group together, but nothing seemed to gel. So, he hustled at his paper routes, took on as much extra paying work as he could shoulder, and played the drums when he had the chance. It was a difficult adjustment to make.

Backyard barbecues sometimes presented opportunities for Bugsy to perform. They were reminiscent of the impromptu affairs in Elizabethtown that Bugsy had attended as a child. Each barbecue was a sweet time, with everybody in a good mood and with plenty to eat. Bugsy was playing one of these affairs in Port Deposit, Maryland, when he noticed a white teenager picking his way through the paper plate–wielding crowd. Another boy, who looked vaguely Asian, followed him. They stood off to the side while Bugsy pushed his playing up a notch behind the pick-up band.

Jackie Lee Madron, Ziggy Soto, and Bernard Purdie made for an unlikely combination: a white guitarist from a local private school, a Hawaiian bass player from a military family stationed at

Bainbridge Naval Base, and a black drummer with a plaid drum set. That was not a typical look for a teenaged musical group in the racially segregated 1950s. Jackie and Ziggy had been looking for a drummer. They were driving within earshot of the music from the barbecue and stopped to get a better listen. Jackie asked Bugsy if he was interested in playing with them, and the group Jackie Lee and the Angels was formed.

Ziggy drove the car. Jackie and Bugsy got the bookings. They played at teenager dances at white Cecil County high schools in Perryville, Havre De Grace, and Northeast and at Catholic church socials on Wednesday nights in Port Deposit. Bugsy secured gigs at Burke's Tavern in Elkton and at other local black nightclubs. Jackie and Ziggy also booked engagements at the naval base enlisted men's club. If dance organizers were initially reluctant to book the trio because of its look, their concerns were quickly overcome by Jackie's assertiveness and Bugsy's charm. Jackie was the lead singer, but Bugsy took to the microphone, too. His humorous rendition of Jimmy Driftwood's "The Battle of New Orleans," popularized by Johnny Horton, was an audience favorite.

> "Yeah they ran through the briars,
> And they ran through the brambles,
> And they ran through the bushes,

Where the rabbits couldn't go.
They ran so fast,
That the hounds couldn't catch 'em,
On down the Mississippi,
To the Gulf of Mexico."[3]

Ironically, it was Bugsy who broadened the group's material to include the country and western songs that he and Mr. Heywood loved so much; if audiences were confused by the group's diverse appearance, the variety of their material must have left them absolutely bewildered. But it was good dance music, and teenagers loved it.

Jackie Lee and the Angels became a local hit. Soon they were working local restaurants that catered to the Chesapeake Bay yachting crowd docked in nearby Chesapeake City, Maryland, including Hillie's and the Island Inn. The group developed a relationship with Jim Fettis, who managed Continental Artists out of his office in Chester, Pennsylvania. (Fettis's office was next door to that of Bill Haley, who was then a local country and western disc jockey.)

The boys joined the local musicians' union in Wilmington, Delaware, and began backing some of the artists that Fettis managed. They even opened for such national acts as Fats Domino,

James Brown and the Famous Flames, Little Richard, Chuck Berry, the Shirrells, Chubby Checker, and Bobby Rydell. This put them in the larger local venues, such as Johnny's Sports Arena in Port Deposit and the Wilmington's National Guard Armory. They almost played on a bill with B.B. King at the Uptown Theater in Philadelphia, but the police detained them only a block from the theater because the trio "looked suspicious." When they eventually arrived at the backstage entrance, B.B. King opened the door and invited them inside. The promoter sent them to wait in the wings, but he never called them out on to the stage.

Bugsy was at last making steady money playing music, but the logistics were more challenging than they had been with Mr. Heywood. Jackie and Ziggy lived close to each other, but Bugsy was twenty miles away, in Elkton. By this time, Mayor Stanley had advanced Bugsy enough money to buy a motor scooter. This made paper deliveries quicker, but Bugsy couldn't carry drums on a motorbike. Because he didn't have practice space for the group in Elkton, Bugsy left his drums in Port Deposit and rode his scooter to practice. Enduring a forty-mile round trip on a motor scooter, exposed to the elements on a cold winter evening, takes real commitment. But Bugsy would never think of canceling or missing a practice. Mr. Heywood had trained him well.

Jackie and Ziggy practically became members of the Purdie family. Jackie remembers Bugsy's relationship with Cap.

"We spent an awful lot of time around Bugsy's family (Cap, his sisters, and his brothers Tommy and Nate), and we all loved Cap to death. He was a nice man. Their mom and dad had passed by that time, I think, so they were literally orphaned, if it hadn't been for Cap and maybe his grandmother, but I think more Cap. He was very quiet. He was very neat, a very neat man. He always had his top button buttoned on his shirt, and he was always dressed nice, and he was very polite and soft-spoken, so he always asked if you were hungry. Cap raised that whole family. I don't think Bugsy will mind me telling you this, but that boy took every penny that he made home and gave it to Cap. I never saw Bugsy buy anything for himself, except if he needed a drumhead or something like that. I never saw that man spend any money. He gave Cap every penny that he had and helped his grandfather raise his sisters."

By his sixteenth birthday, Bugsy had been driving for Stanley for four years. He had driven underage past the Elkton police, the county sheriff, and even the state police, without ever being questioned. But Bugsy was the proudest guy in the world when he finally got his driver's license. Purdie remembers,

"I was sixteen. At 10 o'clock in the morning my driver's license came and I'd go out. I got my driver's license in my hand, and I'm in the car. I'm legal now, and I come down the highway, you know, right down there, go right down the highway and the state police pulled me over. He said, "Boy!" And I'm just grinning from ear to ear.

Uncle Fletch had called a friend at the state police barracks and told the state trooper that Bugsy had just gotten his license. It was Uncle Fletch's farewell to the little boy with no shoes.

Bugsy was growing into adulthood, and women in the clubs where he played began to notice. There was no high school puppy love for Bugsy. He went directly from delivering newspapers on his bicycle to proposing marriage to a woman he met in a Wilmington club who had given birth to his daughter. But she was involved with another man who pushed Bugsy aside, when he returned from the military. He didn't intimidate Bugsy, but he was a grown man, whereasBugsy was still in high school. When the woman rejected Bugsy's proposal, Bugsy reluctantly withdrew from the relationship. He had become a father, but he hadn't started a family of his own.

As Bugsy approached his last year at George Washington Carver School, something began to bother him. The newspapers he had been delivering for the past five years had been filled with front-page headlines about public school desegregation. During the year he started delivering newspapers for Mr. Stanley one headline reported "United States Supreme Court Orders Desegregation of Public Schools." A few years later, another declared, "Eisenhower Sends National Guard into Little Rock." The Maryland papers reported work on a desegregation plan for public schools statewide. Yet he was in his junior year of high school, and not a word was mentioned at George Washington Carver about the plan to desegregate Elkton High School. What was going on? He decided to ask Mayor Stanley. Purdie remembers:

"And Mr. Stanley says, 'Well, Bugsy, why didn't you apply to go?' I said, 'Apply? Apply when?' He said, 'Well, the program has been in effect for two years.' I went immediately to Mrs. Wallace, my sixth-grade teacher and to my guidance teacher. I also went to Mrs. Harriet Fitzgerald, my history teacher, and Mrs. Thelma Bessicks, my first-grade teacher, and I asked each one of them if I could get a letter from them or have them sign on my application to go to the Elkton Senior High School."

With his application approved for September 1959, Bugsy Purdie made history as the first black student to attend and graduate from the previously all-white Elkton High School. All the white students either knew Bugsy or knew someone who knew him. Bugsy was the Negro kid who was the drummer with Jackie Lee and the Angels. Bugsy was their newspaper boy. Bugsy was the shoeshine boy downtown. Bugsy had the whole school as his audience, and he was a bit flamboyant about it. From his newspaper deliveries and collections, he knew most of the families that had children at Elkton High School. But he could not escape the racial taunts and challenges from other boys who wanted to bring him down a peg. Bugsy fought when he felt he had to and accounted for himself well. The bullyboys quickly learned that Bugsy could and would fight them hard. After all, he was one of Jim Purdie's sons. Bugsy knew that if he didn't fight them hard, he would have to go home and fight his own brothers.

Although the principal of George Washington Carver High School had written the Board of Education that Purdie would be class valedictorian if he graduated from that school, Bugsy was, in fact, reading on a seventh-grade level when he entered Elkton High. Yet he applied himself and graduated with the Elkton High School class of 1960. He had no plans to attend college, as that was out of the question, financially, and besides, all he ever wanted to be was a musician.

Mayor Stanley had other plans for Bugsy. William Burkley owned an insurance company in town, the offices of which Bugsy cleaned periodically. More important to Stanley was that Burkley was a member of the Maryland House of Delegates. Stanley talked to Burkley about the chances of Bugsy's getting a state scholarship. It was late in the year, but Burkley thought Bugsy deserved an opportunity to go to college, and the recent high school graduate was offered a work-study scholarship to enroll in business administration at Morgan State College in Baltimore.

Burkley and Stanley drove Bugsy and Cap to Baltimore that August. As the car pulled out on to the southbound lane of Route 40, Bugsy looked back through the rear window to see the spot where he had hustled the marriage trade. He thought about his mother's cooking. She never needed measuring spoons; she did it all by feel, sight, and smell, and she taught him to do the same. Now he was a good cook. He was the first of her children to go to college, but she hadn't lived to see it. For seven years he had slept in the living room chair close to the last place he had seen her alive. In his vigil he would talk to her to let her know that he understood the lessons she had taught him. He would respect his elders. He would get an education. He would make her proud of him.

He thought of his father with that ghastly shotgun wound in his chest. His mind flashed to his first hunting trip with his father. The twelve-gauge shotgun had knocked him to the ground. Would James have been proud of him? Bugsy had always tried to be a real man about things. He'd worked hard to support the family. He'd even stopped drinking.

Then he looked over at old Cap sitting beside him in the backseat of Mr. Burkley's car. Cap. They couldn't have done it without him. They couldn't have kept the family together without his calm, steady hand. Cap was almost 100 years old now, and here he was riding to Baltimore. Suddenly, Cap looked very old and frail.

Mr. Heywood. Where was he? What was he doing? What advice did he have for young Bugsy now? Would Bugsy ever see Mr. Heywood again? Collins Avenue, the farm, Main Street, and the Angels were all receding through the rear window as Burkley wheeled his big sedan south across the Susquehanna River Bridge toward Baltimore.

3.

NIGHTCLUB COLLEGE

Morgan State College was a world apart. The campus sat atop a steep, grassy hill overlooking a broad boulevard in northeastern Baltimore. Morgan was within the city limits, but it was not an urban school in its look or its outlook. On the campus you hardly realized you were in a city. Great stands of mature trees bounded and buffered it from the outside world. Founded in 1867 as the Centenary Biblical Institute, Morgan had long ago broadened its academic curriculum beyond the preparation of its students for the ministry. It had a well-deserved reputation as a progressive institution that attracted some of the best minds of any of the black colleges of its day. Bugsy, who had not faced any serious academic challenges until his senior year of high school, was a complete stranger to this environment.

His childhood nickname returned to Cecil County with Cap, Mayor Stanley and William Burkley. At Morgan he was Bernard Purdie. Bernard started working right away to earn his keep. He became a staff photographer for the school newspaper, and he worked in the school's kitchen. Bernard got to know his new classmates quickly, but he began to realize that in many ways he was not very polished, particularly with Morgan's coeds. He felt like a black hillbilly bumpkin.

But Purdie knew his strengths and immeciately tapped into them. He headed straight for the music department. He tried to change his major to music, but his scholarship wouldn't allow that option until his junior year. So, he joined every student orchestra he could find. Purdie recalls,

"I was well ahead of anyone that played in these bands. I was good. I mean, there were no 'ifs', 'ands,' or 'buts' about it. I knew I was good when it came down to playing the music. So, I didn't have the problem of having to worry about all of the rehearsals that everybody had to do. And on top of everything else, I read music. When I asked them to give me some to read, half the time they didn't have any drum music, so they give me horn parts or the piano parts, and this made things easy for me to follow. I was very, very close to [having] a photographic memory. I knew what it said on the paper. I could take a look at it and could tell you what was on bar 7 and 8. And if I thought I had a problem, I was singing the phrase. I was already down there waiting for that to show up, and for everyone else to get to that point. Then when they'd get there, I knew exactly what I had to play, because I had already been down there playing it in my head. Knowing the relationship and the

emphasis on that bar, I was actually able to play that bar and move the music . . . lift the music, and they just thought that I was like a genius. You know, some more for my ego. Yeah, I had an ego. Ain't no doubt about that. I knew that early in life, but I was good at what I was doing."

Bernard held his own academically in his first semester at Morgan. He kept up with his student jobs and played music. He even gave some thought to the ministry as his calling. He was living with a minister and his family close to the Morgan campus, an arrangement made by Burkley. Some of the folks back home told him he would be a gifted preacher, given his outgoing nature and his gift for gab. Bernard had always been fascinated by the dynamics of the preacher's delivery and his ability to move his congregation. When the preacher needed to make his next car payment, he didn't shout the message at them. Instead, he shouted to prepare them for the message—and when the message came, it came in a whisper. To Bernard this contrast taught him less about God and more about preachers' preoccupation with money. But the example of the preacher's delivery awakened in him the power of subtlety in music: the soft delicate musical phrase, the subtle flourishes, and the grace notes woven into the rhythmic web a musician spins. Bernard was being called to a ministry, but his congregation was not to be found in the church. Rather, it would be in the nightclubs.

There were two Baltimore brothers attending Morgan who could really play. One played trombone and the other trumpet. They and Bernard were kindred musical spirits. The Perry brothers were into the Baltimore nightclub scene, and that's where Bernard wanted to be. The nightclub crowd hungered for good dance music, and that was the music he wanted to play. He wasn't going to be happy until he saw the crowd shimmy to his beats and his rhythms. Bernard had beats that were uniquely his own. His mind had been drawn to them in a thousand different guises. They were all around him. They came at his ears every day—the thump of car tires going over the Conowingo Dam Bridge, the footsteps of mailman Fred back home, the rattles and jingles from Mayor Stanley's van on a cold Sunday morning before sunrise. His mind seized on these everyday noises, and he memorialized them in his playing.

Bernard joined the brothers in the Baltimore nightclubs. It was just the ensemble he'd been looking for: horns, keyboard, singers, guitars, and that good-time crowd looking for a party. The energy in the clubs was exciting, and Bernard stirred it up with a funky flavor all his own. When he wasn't playing with the group, he was in the clubs on his own, begging for a chance to sit in. After he got his chance in one club, he moved on to the next club and sat in there. He was all over the Baltimore club scene as if he were back on Elkton's Main Street, begging for a chance to show what he could do—and when he got his chance, he didn't waste it. He unleashed the full force of his pent-up energy on the music. He opened the throttle and gave his gift full rein. He had the <u>walls</u> shakin'!

Bernard's first semester at Morgan had been manageable, but in his second semester, he began to struggle. Pure memorization didn't give him the ability to move quickly through course material that required elaborate projects or the mastery of complex concepts. Math continued to be a strong subject for him, but his business courses left him cold.

Between his work, his study, and his music, something had to give. He had to work to stay in school and he wanted that college education. He was the first Purdie to go to college; that was important to him. He certainly didn't want to let down Mayor Stanley, William Burkley, Cap, and the many folks in Elkton who had been so supportive of him and his family. He could sense their hope in him, and it weighed on his mind that he was struggling academically. But he was on fire for his music.

Making music playing drums was all he ever really wanted to do. He had a gift, a gift that was driving him away from college. When he was on the bandstand, he was alive in a way that moved his very soul. He couldn't stay away from the clubs. He didn't want to. At some point, he transferred from Morgan State College to the "Nightclub Community College" of Baltimore, with its main campus on Fulton Street and North Avenue. Bernard went to school at the Celebrity Club and The Four Corners, where Redd Fox delivered his bluest material from 2:00 a.m. to 4:00 a.m. on Fridays and Saturdays. The quiet campus at Morgan was fading quickly in his mind. He was marking time there; he knew that he was just delaying the inevitable call to tell the folks back home that he was dropping out of school. But he needed something positive to show them that he was making the right decision and that he merely wasn't running away from the challenge of college work. Purdie men don't run. They stand their ground and fight. He had to make a mark in music before he made that call.

Bernard completed his spring semester on a steady diet of required courses, required work, and as many club engagements as he could manage. He stayed in Baltimore that summer to work on campus, and without classes, he was able to play full time. He hit the clubs hard. If he wasn't playing a set engagement, he was begging for a chance to sit in. He would tell anyone who would listen about his musical pedigree. He knew all the big names: Count Basie, Duke

LET THE DRUMS SPEAK!

Ellington, Joe Jones, Sonny Greer, Lloyd Price, James Brown. He'd opened for them at Johnny's Sports Arena in Port Deposit. They'd heard him play. He was good. Bernard gave the clubs the hard sell and, though skeptical, they'd let him on the band stand. Then he'd go to work showing what he could do. After leaving the bandstand in one club, he'd move to the next club and beg for a chance to sit in there. He hustled tirelessly for playing time each night until the clubs closed.

As Bernard's reputation grew quickly in Baltimore musical circles, he worked as much as he could. One night he entered a small store in the club district. The clerk asked if he wouldn't mind waiting a few minutes before ringing up the order while the owner ran an errand. A few minutes went by, and the owner returned with a policeman, pointing at Bernard and saying, "There he is! He's one of them!" The policeman arrested Bernard, put him in a police cruiser, and took him to jail. Bernard was dumbfounded and afraid. He'd been to the Elkton jail many times to run errands for the sherriff, but despite Juicy Kaplan's friendly manner toward him, he had always been afraid of the cells and the enforced indolence of the confinement. Perhaps the inmates there were just having fun with a credulous little boy when they warned Bugsy about the horrors of prison life, but he had believed them—and those warnings were haunting him now that he was locked up in a Baltimore jail cell.

Bernard needed help. He had hoped to call home soon to tell everyone he was on his way to a promising career as a professional musician. Instead, he was forced to call home in shame to ask for help because he was in jail for robbery. Burkley retained a Baltimore lawyer to represent Bernard. At his court appearance, the lawyer pled Bernard's good character as a Morgan student and a favorite son of Elkton. The judge dismissed the charges with a stern warning to Bernard to be careful of the company he kept in the future. The musical brothers he had been playing with—being drug addicts—had robbed the store. Bernard had not been involved in the robbery and had not known of the crime, but he was closely associated with the brothers, and that association had almost wrecked him.

Bernard's arrest shook him. He had escaped the charges, but he started to question how he was going to break into the music business from Baltimore. All the big-time players were working out of New York. Baltimore had been a compromise because he was in school there. He might have left for New York that fall, but having gotten help with the lawyer from Burkley, he couldn't very well say "Thank you" and then just quit school. He determined to stick with his original plan and try to make his mark before calling home to tell everybody that he was leaving school.

Gathering the other musicians, he had played with in the Perry brothers' group, Bernard started a group of his own. He moved out of the reverend's house and into a room with another musician and started hustling for gigs full time. It was his group now, and he began to run it the way Clyde Bessicks led his orchestra. The musicians didn't read music, but Bernard had the music tucked away in that computer-like mind of his; he drilled the group at rehearsals on the precision of their playing and the nuances of their ensemble work. When they were ready, he would take them to New York and make his mark. He started talking it up. All thoughts of Morgan were behind him.

And so it came to be that one morning at 2:00 a.m., an old sedan with a small trailer attached to its bumper stood parked in the alley behind the club where the Bernard Purdie Band was playing. It hadn't been easy to convince his band to strike out for New York, but Bernard was persistent. They were all skeptical that, as complete unknowns, they could just show up in New York City and find work. Ross, the guitar player, had an uncle in the Bronx, and Bernard seized on his New York connection to convince the others of the feasibility of what he wanted to do. Besides, Bernard himself had connections with New York musicians from his days with Mr.

Heywood. When any of the big bands came through Baltimore, he would be at the stage door, renewing acquaintances. They still remembered little Bugsy from Elkton, and they encouraged him. Ross finally asked his uncle to give the band a place to stay in New York. One by one, the obstacles faded away. The band was still skeptical, but Bernard was so sure of himself and of the success that they would enjoy that they decided to roll the dice.

The last set of the night came to an end, and the diehard patrons slowly shuffled out of the club. Bernard's voice was filled with excitement as he hustled to break down his drum set and get to the car before any of the other musicians had a last-minute change of heart. The streets were practically deserted as the overloaded sedan pulled out of the alley with the five musicians and most of their worldly possessions bound for New York City. Heading toward Philadelphia, the car turned northward on to Route 1 and into the Pennsylvania farmland. They all tried to appear matter of fact about the trip, but it was a big step. Deep into the early morning, they passed through the upper section of Philadelphia along Roosevelt Boulevard and then crossed the Delaware River at Trenton, New Jersey. With little traffic, they made good time and reached the George Washington Bridge at sunrise Monday morning. The sight of the New York skyline lifted their spirits, but at the base of those majestic skyscrapers lay many broken dreams.

PART II
MAKIN' IT

4.

NO LOOKING BACK

In the early morning hours, the members of Bernard's band meandered through the Bronx looking for the apartment building where Ross's uncle worked as the superintendent and also lived with his family. When they finally found it, the morning rush hour had started. Ross's uncle helped the fellows unload their bags and instruments. Across the street from the apartment building was a bar called the Comet Club. Ross's uncle had talked to the club's owner about his nephew's band coming up to New York from Baltimore. When he saw the musical instruments, the owner came over to the car and asked the band if they wanted to audition that morning. The guys then took their instruments from the car into the Comet Club and set up. That night they were to play their first set in New York City.

Monday nights were slow for clubs, and this Monday night was no exception. Even so, the band caused a stir among the patrons who did come out that night. This new band from Baltimore was tight and funky. The musicians could tell they were making a strong impression. They couldn't believe that just the night before, they were virtual unknowns, and tonight they were causing some excitement in a city that was used to hearing the hottest groups in the entertainment business. Maybe Bernard had been right all along. Maybe stardom was just a matter of being willing to put yourself out there. The owner seemed excited and put a sign in the window announcing the New York debut of the hot new band from Baltimore. The bartender talked about getting some music heavyweights over to hear the group. Things seemed to be moving very quickly. It was a Cinderella story in the making.

Every night the audience got bigger, and the buzz over the group and its prospects intensified. On Thursday night Sylvia Vanderpool came to the Comet Club. The single "Love Is Strange" had hit number one on the R&B charts in 1957, and the haunting guitar voicings of Mickey Baker emulating a bewitched lover's trance induced by Sylvia Vanderpool's provocative delivery, "Come here, my little lover boy," still knocked audiences out. The band knew she was there, and every musician was focused. Of course, the band played the song well that night. She was definitely impressed. Four nights in New York and they were getting a serious look from a top act. This was what they had come to New York for, but no one had expected things to happen so quickly.

The band had even been able to cover the absence of the saxophone player. He'd suddenly gotten homesick and taken a train back to Baltimore. The funny thing was that he didn't even tell anyone. He just left the Comet Club on a break and didn't come back. He left his saxophone on the bandstand, walked to the subway, rode to Penn Station, and went home. The show went on, with the fellows figuring it out later. When they called back to Baltimore, there he was. He'd gone home to be with his girlfriend. As Ross put it, "Ain't nothing wrong with that nigger. That girl done got to him again."

The energy of the late-week New York club crowd was intoxicating, and the band was expecting it only toget better on the weekend. Sylvia Vanderpool returned to the Comet Club to listen to the band rehearse. She left the club midway through the rehearsal, and when it was over, the bartender called Purdie over to talk to him. Then Purdie huddled with the band. What was Sylvia's verdict? Well, Mickey and Sylvia were going into Bell Sound Studios that Sunday to re-record "Love Is Strange." The guys smiled at each other, that is, all except Purdie. They only wanted him for the recording session, not the whole band. Purdie tried to put the best face on things. They only needed a drummer for that particular session. He was sure they would want the whole band in the future. But it was obvious they were disappointed. The band played Friday night and Saturday night at the Comet Club, but it wasn't the same. On Sunday the band announced to Purdie that they were going back to Baltimore.

Purdie was determined to stay. He played on the Sunday afternoon recording session and made eighty dollars, more money than he had ever made for a single engagement. He called home and told everyone he had gotten his big break in music in New York. Purdie gushed with excitement as he explained himself over the phone. He had just recorded with Mickey and Sylvia, a duo with a number-one hit record. He'd made more money than he had ever seen at one time in his life for just one afternoon of work. They liked his playing and wanted him to stay in New York. This was his big chance to do what he always wanted to do, and he just <u>had</u> to take it. He was leaving Morgan to pursue music full time. He loved to play, and he was going to be the best drummer in the world. Cap, Mayor Stanley, and William Burkley had hoped Bugsy would finish his education, but they also understood that this was his dream. If this was what he really wanted to do, they agreed that he should pursue it. They all wished him well.

Purdie had officially cut his tether to Elkton. He was on his own now in the recording capital of the world. It was up to him to make his dream a reality. Although his band had deserted him, he was off to a quick start. He would start another band, but now it was time to celebrate. So, he spent the recording session money like a sailor on Shanghai shore leave, and after a day or two, he was broke. Purdie had no band and no job, but he did have prospects. It was time for him to pursue them. He was going to have to hustle main street New York City just like he had hustled Main Street Elkton—except in Manhattan it was called Broadway. He had to figure out how to get from the Bronx to Broadway.

Joe Robinson wasn't the mayor, but he knew his way around New York. He was Sylvia Vanderpool Robinson's husband and co-owner of Sylvia's Blue Morocco on Boston Post Road. Robinson liked Purdie and thought it was time for him to hear some plain talk about trying to make it as a session player in New York. Joe sat Purdie down at his club and told him the facts of life. Purdie had talent, but if he wanted to do session work, he needed to be downtown where the studios were. And he needed a day job. That money Purdie had been paid for the Sunday session was not the norm for a musician just starting out. It would be a while before he saw money like that for a single session. The most he could expect was ten dollars a session for doing demo records, and he would have to hustle just to get that meager amount. But demo records would give him exposure; if he stayed with it, he could eventually do major sessions with full orchestrations for good money. But that kind of work was given to established session players. Purdie would have to work his way into those jobs.

Joe gave him an address downtown and told him to see the manager to ask for a job. The address was not for a studio. It was for the Globe Laundry at 49th Street and 10th Avenue. The pay wasn't great, but he could make his rent. Purdie also needed to check out three clubs near the laundry where session players hung out—Jack Dempsey's, Beefsteak Charlie's, and The Turf Club. Meanwhile, he could sit in with the band at the Blue Morocco, and when he got his own band together, Joe would see that they got to play there as well. He gave Purdie $30 and sent him on his way.

Purdie took the subway downtown and found the Globe Laundry on 49th Street near the Hudson River. It was a huge operation. Tractor-trailers with giant commercial loads of towels, sheets, and assorted linens from hotels as far away as Connecticut crammed the loading dock. Laundry workers wheeled large, canvas-sided dollies in and out of the cavernous trailers like they were mining coal. Across the loading dock, gluttonous washing machines consumed the laundry. It required the full strength of one man just to open and close one washing machine door. The trucks kept coming, and the workers kept the dollies moving in an endless river of wash. Purdie told the manager that Joe Robinson had sent him, and, "presto"—Purdie had a job loading sheets and pillowcases into the washing machines from 7:00 a.m. to 4:30 in the afternoon. It was backbreaking manual labor, the kind of work his father had reveled in.

For Bernard, it was a means to an end. He was buying time until he could show New York what he could do—what he was born to do. Even in the big Manhattan laundry room, rhythm was never far from his mind. Work has a rhythm, whichPurdie had always found and expressed. Soon he was dancing and jiving his way through his shift with his own adaptation of a field holler. The tractor-trailers were his backstage, and the canvas laundry carts his props. It was hot, funky work, but around Purdie, you'd think it was a party.

After work Purdie headed for the musicians' clubs. There he found the anteroom to the world of the session musician. That eighty dollars had ruined him. He had his eye set on doing studio work full time, and here was where he had to start. If Baltimore was Nightclub College, then these midtown Manhattan musicians' clubs were Purdie's graduate school of session work. He changed out of his sweat-soaked clothes from the laundry into more dapper attire and walked confidently to the strip of musician hangouts a few blocks away. He entered the first one, and as his eyes adjusted to the gloomy darkness, he realized he was getting the once-over by a good part of the room. He was sticking out like the outsider he was. That kind of thing never bothered Purdie. He was there for only one thing: to get as much studio work as he could get as fast as he could get it. The rest didn't matter. He went to the bar and discreetly ordered a Shirley Temple. He'd learned from experience that the club bartender is the avenue for breaking into a new scene, and it didn't do to flaunt the consumption of soft drinks at the bar. He ran a tab and took in as much as he could from the conversations around him.

There seemed to be very little talk about music and a lot of interest in off-track betting. He didn't recognize anyone he knew. He was beginning to wonder if he'd come to the right place. There was no live music. This was obviously not a playing situation. There was a session musician pecking order in this town, and he needed to learn what it was, who was at the top of it, and how he could break into it. Purdie couldn't break into it on his reputation. He had none in New York. He'd recorded on a number-one hit song, but that was on a remake, not on the original. Musicians with promise were a dime a dozen in New York. They were here today and gone tomorrow. He wasn't going to brag his way into the studio. He would keep his ears open and bide his time.

But Purdie was not passive about going after something he wanted. For him it was the James Purdie philosophy: work three jobs, stay in constant motion, and be ready for anything. Playing the music was never a problem for him. He had absolute confidence in his musical ability. He was never in doubt about what needed to be done in a piece of music, whether on a stage or in a studio. But ability was no guarantee of success. He had to make something happen.

He went back to the Comet Club and started to audition musicians for a new band, one that would be molded according to his own musical instincts. That kind of creative control excited him. He set out to organize a dance band to play the Comet Club, Sylvia's Blue Morocco, and other dinner and dance clubs in the city. It would be a cover band performing a wide range of material, from calypso and R&B to Latin and country & western. The players had to commit to a rigorous schedule of rehearsals and would need to learn material to fill four forty-five-minute sets without repeating a single composition. No one in the audience was likely to be there for all four sets, but the waitresses and the bartenders would be in the club all night, and they would have as much to do with spreading the word about the new band as anyone.

While Purdie organized his own band through auditions at the Comet Club, he played with Les Cooper's band. Cooper was the booking agent for the Comet Club. His band played Thursday through Sunday nights in a separate back room where the club charged admission. A native of Norfolk, Virginia, Les Cooper had established a reputation in New York's doo-wop scene, playing a honky-tonk piano style behind such local groups as The Empires and The Whirlers before forming his own group, The Soul Rockers. Mickey Baker also occasionally called on Purdie to play drums with his band at the Blue Morocco. In addition to being known for his vocals with Sylvia Vanderpool Robinson, Mickey Baker was one of the most sought-after studio guitarists in New York. Baker was a guitarist on countless sessions for Atlantic Records, King, RCA, Decca, and Okeh in the 1950s. As a guitarist, Baker had backed the Drifters on "Money Honey" and "What a Night"; Joe Turner on "Shake Rattle and Roll"; Ruth Brown on "Momma, He Treats Your Daughter Mean"; and Big Maybelle on "A Whole Lotta Shakin' Goin' On." It's Baker's voice (usually assumed to be Ike Turner's) on Ike and Tina Turner's first hit record "It's Gonna' Work Out Fine." Purdie was sure that Mickey Baker was the key to breaking into the recording studios in a big way.[4]

Purdie recognized that the Blue Morocco was more upscale than the Comet Club. It drew a more affluent clientele with a heavy representation of numbers bankers. The club could afford to bring in bigger acts such as Bobby Hebb, Lloyd Price, and Chuck Jackson, and it consequently demanded a higher level of musicianship from any group seeking to play there. As a performer, the versatile Hebb was compared to Sammy Davis, Jr. He was also a prolific songwriter whose composition "Sunny" remains one of the most frequently performed songs ever penned.

Purdie would need a better band than he had brought from Baltimore to make it into the Blue Morocco and the bigger New York clubs. Even if Joe Robinson let him on stage with a lesser unit, Purdie knew a poor showing would be disastrous. He had to be ready before he tackled the Blue Morocco with his own group. There was no shortage of good New York musicians, but not many good musicians were willing to rehearse with a new band without pay and Purdie couldn't afford to pay for rehearsals. He could at least represent that the Comet Club would give his group work when they were ready, and the prospect of playing at Sylvia's Blue Morocco was also a draw. But most musicians wanted to play and get paid, not invest several months in rehearsal to play at the Comet Club. The music was never the issue. Purdie could teach his players the music. His challenge was finding musicians willing to invest their time in a new venture.

Purdie maintained a consistent routine. He worked at the Globe Laundry until 4:30 p.m. and then headed straight for the musicians' clubs to look for session work. By 6:30 p.m., he was back in the Bronx at the Comet Club for auditions for his new band. In the late evening, he was on the bandstand with Les Cooper's or Mickey Baker's band or sitting in wherever he could. Gradually, Purdie was able to build a new unit.

"I couldn't afford to put the band together to play anywhere, so we had to rehearse and learn songs. So, this is what I had to find first, somebody who did not mind rehearsing. I found Jewel Page on the bass and vocal. Now, all she could do was rock. And then Ray Schinnery, guitar. He did nothing but blues and calypso, but he did sing. And then there was Jimmy Chisholm. He was a jazz saxophone player. In the beginning I tried to get Bill Bivens on saxophone, but Bill was too busy. And because I didn't pressure him, he said, 'Well, you know, whenever I can, I'll come and join you.' So that worked out, and that took, I'd say from three to six months before I would take a job because we had to learn some songs. By the time we took a job we knew thirty songs, I would say thirty songs, that we could actually play as a band." – Bernard Purdie

It was an eclectic group, but they were willing to work hard for an unknown musician who had been in New York less than a month.

Even though Bill Bivens wasn't a regular with his band, he became one of Purdie's closest friends.

"Bill and I go back to almost the first month or two that I came into New York. I saw him play in a club, and I took a liking to his sound. I didn't have any gigs except working at the Comet, and he'd sit in once in a while, but he was already working for Ross Carnegie, especially on the weekends. Bill's mother used to cook. She was a big, big cook. So, a lot of musicians used to come and hang around Bill's house. It was right around the corner from where I lived." – Bernard Purdie

Bivens introduced Purdie to the hottest clubs and the hottest bands in the city.

". . . the High Hat, the Hideout, the 845 Club, and the Boston Ballroom. See, these were what we called the big clubs. And then you had Small's Paradise, you had Count Basie's, you had the Lenox Lounge, you had Lenox Terrace, before you went downtown to where you got to 52nd Street, which was in the cellar, where you had the Jazz Room. Then you had Minton's Playhouse on 118th Street."

At that time, King Curtis had the hottest band, and Ed Smalls had the hottest club, Small's Paradise at 135th Street and Eighth Avenue in Harlem. Opened in 1920, Small's was an institution in the New York club scene. In 1960 Wilt Chamberlain joined Ed Small in the club, and it was renamed Wilt's Small's Paradise. The Fort Worth, Texas, tenor saxophone sound of King Curtis spawned legions of copycats. Curtis's musicianship was impeccable as an instrumentalist and as a composer and arranger. He was a shrewd businessman and ran a first-class outfit. Most importantly, Curtis was the musical director for the most significant label in the history of rhythm and blues, Atlantic Records. At Small's one night, Bivens introduced Purdie to Curtis as an up-and-coming drummer in the city. Of course, Purdie wanted to sit in that night, but Curtis was cool to the idea. You couldn't hurt Purdie's feelings, and he was determined to keep coming back to Small's until Curtis gave him a shot. King Curtis was king of the hill, and that was where Purdie wanted to be. As Purdie saw it, that was where he was <u>supposed</u> to be—at the top.

Despite his early successes, there was no easy route to where Purdie wanted to go. He was working at the Globe Laundry, hustling for studio work, playing nights and weekends with his own band, and keeping up his contacts for more work and better opportunities. Then he got a scare. He was working the big washing machines at the laundry when a machine door weighing over two hundred pounds nearly crushed his hand. He was rushed to the hospital, where they placed his hand in a cast. Yet Purdie was determined that nothing was going to stand in the way of his playing. After several weeks the cast was removed, and Purdie started playing again. Perhaps it was carelessness or fatigue, but something had to give at the pace he was keeping. When Purdie felt more confident about his income from music, he would leave the laundry. He didn't have long to wait. Several months later he went on the road for a two-week engagement in the Boston area with a local saxophonist named Lonnie Youngblood. When he returned, he gave notice to the Globe Laundry that he was leaving to play music full time. He was told that he would always have a job there if he needed one, but Purdie would never return. Purdie hadn't made it in the music business yet, but the era of needing a day job was over for him.

* * * *

Les Cooper wasn't a studio heavyweight, but he had recorded on several small labels. When he was recording again on Bobby and Danny Robinson's Everlast Label (on which King Curtis and the Noble Knights recorded "Soul Twist"), he put Purdie in the studio on drums. After the recording session, Purdie had taken up with Youngblood, but one of Cooper's singles hit the charts in October of 1962. "Wiggle Wobble" stayed on the charts for sixteen weeks, topping out at number 22. Cooper followed up the popularity of

"Wiggle Wobble" with a tour down the Atlantic seaboard to Jacksonville, Florida. Cooper hired Purdie away from Youngblood for his tour. Purdie and the rest of the Soul Rockers shoehorned themselves into Cooper's new Cadillac for a road trip that took them through the heart of the South.

"We hit Baltimore, Washington . . . we hit Havre de Grace, we hit in Virginia, West Virginia, Georgia, Atlanta. We hit all of the towns going down, but we got escorted out of every town that we went through." – Bernard Purdie

Five black men in a new Cadillac with New York tags pulling a trailer through the South were an easy target for every enterprising law man along the route, so Cooper kept plenty of cash to lubricate the wheels of justice as the miles clicked by. It wasn't quite a national tour, but it was a significant set of engagements, and Purdie made sure everyone back home knew about the record and the tour. When Les Cooper and The Soul Rockers hit Havre de Grace, half of Elkton showed up. Even mailman Fred went to the concert. Purdie was all smiles the whole night.

Purdie's dream of fame was no longer pie-in-the-sky; it was starting to come true. He just needed to build on his good fortune. "Wiggle Wobble" was Purdie's first hit record. There were excellent musicians who had struggled in New York for years and never played on even one hit. Purdie had come out of nowhere and scored a hit within six months. Still, the record companies were not breaking down his door to get him to play on their sessions. Purdie was determined to build a reputation that would get him steady work in the major studios.

After the "Wiggle Wobble"Tour, Purdie went back to building his own band. It took several months, but gradually one started to gel. The band rehearsed at the Comet Club and performed there until Purdie felt they were ready for deeper waters. Eventually he worked his band into the bigger Bronx clubs: the Hideout, the Boston Ballroom, the 845 Club, the Lenox Lounge, the Lenox Terrace, the Hideaway, the High Hat, and the Blue Morocco. Purdie had a game plan, and he stuck to it. He moved his band from club to club, never staying in any one venue more than two months, no matter how comfortable the situation. The regular customers tire of the same sound after a while, and the band becomes stale, even if it continues to add new material.

"I was working five, six, and seven days a week, because I formed the group, and we were doing things in these places. We'd sign a contract [for] two-weeks with a two-week option—always staying just about— each one of them we ended up staying almost two months because in two months' time, I was already booked to be in

another club [with] the same kind of thing. Two weeks with two-week options. So, I was regular. I had good jobs. I always had a good band and was always working. Once in a while, in one of the clubs, we'd have Tuesday off. We wouldn't start until Wednesday, go Wednesday through Sunday, and do a double on Saturday. But we worked five, six, and seven nights a week, and on the one night we usually had off, which was on Mondays, those are jam sessions going someplace, so we always went to that. So, I was never home, not in the evenings, always out in a club someplace."
– Bernard Purdie

Purdie played the Bronx dance clubs at night and on the weekends, but during the week, he went downtown to circulate in the musicians' clubs in midtown Manhattan. Now that he had left the Globe Laundry, he went to the clubs early in the morning. Even at that hour, he found musicians at the bar with drinks in their hands. At the clubs he was dubbed "Mississippi Big Foot" by a tenor saxophonist named Buddy Lucas. When Purdie entered the club, he could count on seeing Lucas's six-foot-four frame at the bar. Lucas would wheel around on his stool and exclaim, "Well, if it isn't Mississippi Big Foot!" That was Purdie's cue to come to the bar and pay his respects. Lucas liked Purdie and tried to help him to the extent he could, but Purdie was going to have to pay his own dues before he would gain any respect as a legitimate studio drummer. Indeed, Purdie had played on "Wiggle Wobble," but he had not become known in the circle of musicians who specialized in studio work. He was about to learn the difference between a musician who makes records—even hit records—and a studio musician who is hired to come into a recording session cold and make a hit, often out of new material that was based on written arrangements, and in a situation in which the hourly cost of the session places a premium on getting the job done well and done quickly.

Lucas introduced Purdie to a number of musicians, and Purdie introduced himself to anyone else who would listen to his pitch. He bought drinks, and with the drinks came information but no work. Everyone was polite. They would keep him in mind. Purdie kept going to the clubs every day, as though it were his day job. Gradually, his eyes were opened to the reality of a world about which he had dreamed but about which he knew very little.

The musicians' clubs held a microcosm of the world of the popular musician. There were the club players, who were wholly adequate for playing in bands, orchestras, and musical groups. They played locally as well as going on the road. They played in dance bands and behind vocalists and singing groups. The fortunate club players found themselves in music groups with hit records and large popular followings. If a musician found himself in that kind of situation, he might become famous and wealthy. For the most part, though, these musicians were instrumentalists and backup singers. The popularity of vocalists was a sore point with instrumentalists, many of whom had spent long, arduous hours of practice to hone their musical skills to a fine edge, only to find themselves eclipsed in the public mind by singers, who often became successful based more on good looks than musical ability. It was the instrumentalists who had been in the vanguard of popular music for decades. The bandleaders and soloists had originally been the stars, while the singers had been relegated to cameo appearances. It's hard to say why the vocalists eclipsed the instrumentalists as the artists whom fans came to worship. Perhaps it was the technology of microphones. Perhaps it was the successful promotion of larger-than-life personalities. A singer could sing, dance, act, and tell jokes in the same show, but whoever paid money to see a dancing saxophonist? Instrumentalists were tied to their instruments. They were one with their instruments, and they served the music they loved with an almost monkish devotion. As they saw it, the instrumentalists were the true musicians and, with rare exception, the vocalists were just along for the ride—but getting most of the glory and the money.

Then there were the session musicians. Session players were hired to play on record dates. They also played in clubs, in bands, and on the road, in addition to backing up vocalists, but they also were excellent readers. Great technique was expected of these musicians, as was the ability to master material on the spot and to give record producers what they wanted, when they wanted it. These players were the cream of the musical crop, although they weren't necessarily well known to the general public. Club musicians possessing modest reading skills who tried to enter the ranks of the session players were quickly found out. You only got one chance, and if you screwed up, you were history. The producers never forgot, nor did the contracting musician who vouched for a slacker who hadn't cut it on a studio date. Players in the rhythm section could ease themselves into session work a little more gradually than could horn players.

Drummers, bass players, rhythm guitarists, and keyboard players were called to make demo recordings. Demos were produced in abbreviated recording sessions with minimal instrumentation as an aid to deciding whether to invest in a more costly, full-scale production of a major record date. Demos were generally recorded in the morning and early afternoons, while the major recording sessions were held in the late afternoons and early evenings. When Purdie started circulating in the musicians' clubs earlier in the day, he noticed the presence of players he had never seen when he would arrive in the late afternoon, after his shift at the laundry. These clubs functioned almost like informal hiring halls, in which arrangers and contract musicians would come in looking for drummers or guitarists or other instrumentalists to fill out a session or to line one up for a future date. The demo musicians would roll out of the clubs earlier in the day, and the major session players would roll in to wait for the studios to open for their dates. Purdie tried to get to know the contracting musicians who both played on recording dates and hired other musicians for those dates. He also tried to get to know the arrangers, usually keyboard players, in the hopes of getting work through them, but arrangers didn't do much hanging out at these clubs, since they were always busy working on compositions.

Purdie kept hustling for work to keep his band busy and build his own reputation. He was always eager for any news that might help him get into the studio. That meant not only going to the musicians' clubs daily but also hanging out after his own gigs and going to hear other groups play, sitting in when he could. One important contact he made was Sticks Evans, a left-handed studio drummer who taught music in the New York public schools and who took on private students. Purdie became one of Evans's students with the goal of improving his ability to sight-read music. He studied with Evans for six months; at the end of his training, he was able to read a half page ahead of the passage he was playing.

LET THE DRUMS SPEAK!

One afternoon Purdie was at The Turf Club with Buddy Lucas, when an excited contract musician came in, looking for a drummer to play on a demo. Purdie jumped up immediately, claiming, "I can do it!" The musician ignored him. Lucas spoke up, "Aw, give Mississippi Big Foot a chance." The musician left the club, with Purdie followinghim out the door, insisting, "I can do it! Just give me a chance! I can do it!" The musician went into Jack Dempsey's. He found no drummers there. Purdie was still following him, begging for a chance, and reeling off a laundry list of his accomplishments and his abilities. The musician went into Beefsteak Charlie's and found no drummer there, either. Purdie followed him into and out of the third club, pleading with him. The musician ignored Purdie, but he didn't say no. Purdie followed him down 52nd Street to 1650 Broadway and into a doorway leading down to a basement recording studio. While the musician went into the sound booth to tell the record producer that he couldn't find a drummer, Purdie sat down at the drum set.

The other musicians, not knowing what was going on, ran down the tune with Purdie, and Purdie started to play. What prompted Purdie to pick up his brushes and play them on an R&B tune is anyone's guess. Perhaps it was just his musical instinct honed after so many years of playing and longing. The use of brushes in rhythm and blues was completely unorthodox, but Purdie played brushes anyway. And while the producer, Artie Ripp, and the contracting musician, bassist Barney Richmond, argued in the control booth, the song unfolded like a flower blossoming. The session included Ernie Hayes on organ, Wally Richardson on guitar, and Bob Bushnell on electric bass, playing an arrangement by Horace Ott. Ripp stopped arguing with Richmond and told the engineer to cut on the tape. The recording was done in ten minutes. Purdie left the studio without getting paid. He had to get up to the Bronx for a rehearsal. Richmond didn't even know Purdie's name. He had to track him down through Buddy Lucas to pay him.

It was a nice tune, but many demos are never released. The record producer decided to set up a master recording session based on the demo but did not call Purdie to play on it. Yet, when the master recording was attempted, the producer realized that the demo was better. Whatever had happened in the studio when recording the demo had not been reproduced in the more elaborate master session, so Atlantic Records released the demo as a single, and in June of 1963 it entered the Billboard charts and went to number 10 on the pop chart. The record, "Just One Look," cowritten by American R&B singers Doris Troy and Gregory Carroll and sung by Doris, would be the only hit record of her career.

5.

KING CURTIS

Purdie was knocking at the gate of Emerald City, and that gate was about to open for him. It was a city with a musical history on which Purdie was determined to make his mark— to be recognized as the top studio drummer in New York. Indeed, he intended to win recognition as the greatest drummer in the world. He was confident of his musical ability, and he was tenacious. He would reach those lofty heights as a studio musician. As he saw it, studio work was the most demanding job to excel at consistently.

A studio musician was called for a session cold—with no rehearsal—and was expected to produce a superb rendition on the spot. His sight-reading had to be impeccable, yet at the same time, he was expected to depart from the written music as necessary to elevate the performance. Often there was no written drum part, so he would interpret his part from the piano or horn chart.

Each record producer worked differently. Some welcomed input from studio players, taking a more collaborative approach, while others were put off by it. Making even modest musical suggestions at a session required tact, lest the producer resent the advice. After all, the studio musician was a hired hand summoned there to do as he or she was told. He had no financial stake in the commercial success of the recording except by way of enhancing his own reputation by playing on a hit record. The arrangement was strictly fee for service. In any case, Purdie, by his own admission, had a big mouth and was very opinionated on matters affecting the rhythm section and the rhythmic feel of the piece. Whether it was politics or not, Purdie was going to speak his mind. He was a country boy, but he wasn't a bashful one.

Purdie was always on fire for the music. He couldn't hold back, even if he wanted to. But his assertiveness went beyond his love of performing. He was representing. He was representing his father, whose work ethic was legendary. He was representing his mother, who he believed was looking down on him and would be pleased that he was doing great things. He was representing Cap, his brothers and sisters, Mr. Heywood, Mayor Stanley, and the people of Elkton who had supported him and his family in the difficult years. Purdie knew his strengths. He would outplay the competition, outwork them, and outlast them. He set his sights on the top New York drummers.

The highest paid drummers were on staff at the television networks, for example, Gordon "Specs" Powell at Columbia Broadcasting System who played under the brilliant and eccentric musical director Raymond Scott. Among other shows, Powell played The

Ed Sullivan Show. A New York native from Harlem, Powell was one of the first black musicians on staff at any of the television networks. Powell's income was reportedly in six figures even in the early 1960s. He also did studio work. But the most in-demand session drummer at the time was Panama Francis. Born in Miami, Florida, from the age of thirteen Francis had made his living playing the drums. An accomplished big band jazz drummer, he had played with Cab Calloway's band at the famous Savoy Ballroom. When the music changed in the 1950s, Panama Francis changed with it, establishing himself as the drummer of choice for many of the popular records of the new musical era. Purdie was determined to be the heir to the Panama Francis's throne in the world of New York session drummers.

Talented instrumental musicians arrive in New York City every day with dreams of stardom, and every day just as many leave with their dreams in tatters. The old musical heads can spot these dreamers coming from a mile away, and they know how to shrink their big heads down to size. Purdie's head was growing pretty wide, but he didn't see it that way. "It ain't braggin' if you can back it up," he told himself. In those days Purdie was cutting a pretty wide swath in musical circles as a rookie. After all, he had come to New York not knowing a soul and in less than a week he was in the studio with a top act. He'd also recorded Les Cooper's biggest hit,

"Wiggle Wobble," that same year, and now he had made a national hit out of a $10 demo job that was so good the studio issued and promoted the record "as is." At Sylvia's Blue Morocco, he was backing up Mickey Baker, currently at the top of the heap of studio guitarists. Purdie was running with the big dogs, and he knew it. He was heading for the big time as fast as his chops and reading skills could carry him.

One afternoon Purdie ran into Panama Francis coming into Beefsteak Charlie's and blurted out, "I'm going to take your job!" Francis seemed flabbergasted and began to stutter. Purdie was taken aback by this reaction. Later, he learned that Francis had a speech impediment. Word of this encounter spread quickly among studio musicians; the next time Purdie came into the club, Herb Lovelle grabbed him by his arm and rudely pushed him into a booth in back. Lovelle, a top studio drummer himself, gave Purdie a piece of his mind about what he had done. Lovelle told him that the business wasn't about competing to take anyone's job. There were plenty of studios recording at the same time, and Purdie couldn't possibly play in all of them simultaneously. You help the next guy get a job, and he helps you. Otherwise, they were all going to lose out, because despite what he might think, black session players were just barely getting calls anyway. Purdie listened to Lovelle, believed him, and felt ashamed of how he had treated Francis. He hadn't given him the respect that he was due. Francis, being from an earlier generation, was what his mother had called an elder, and Purdie had vowed to respect his elders.

If it had been anyone else, that kind of assertiveness would have been deemed so obnoxious that no one would have wanted to work with him. But Purdie was young, and there was sincerity in his manner, which softened his headlong rush into things. Purdie was naïve in numerous ways, so rather than put him in his place, the older and more experienced musicians forgave a lot in him. As they would often say, "Purdie's just being Purdie." It had the same cadence as, "Aw, let him go to the church picnic." Also, Purdie was—as Ray Charles once described himself—"raw-assed country." There was no guile in Purdie. He was charming in his own special way, and most people just liked him right off the bat. He was a personification of his own playing: positive, upbeat, and optimistic. His love for music infected everyone around him. He was fun to be around. He made you feel good. His playing made you feel good. You couldn't get him down.

Purdie must have made his peace with Francis Panama because Francis chose Purdie as his understudy in the 1963 musical Marathon 33, starring Julie Harris. Purdie was thrilled. He had always emphasized his reading skills; "I can read anything! I can play any style!" he would say, without taking a breath so he could get it all in. A theatrical job, even as a backup, was a big vote of confidence for Purdie. The lead drummer isn't going to recommend anyone as his understudy who is going to jeopardize his reputation. Purdie would have a full score to work with, not just sketchy charts and half-arranged material. This would be a real test for Purdie, but one he had every confidence he would pass with flying colors—and he did. He rehearsed with the pit orchestra, whichreminded him of his days back in Cecil County playing in the circus band. The performers, the conductor, and a score cued to the action made for a different and yet familiar environment. Produced by the Actors Studio under the supervision of Lee Strasberg, the studio's artistic director, the play was set at a 1933 dance marathon in a midwestern town. Julie Harris played a vaudevillian named June. It wasn't long before Purdie's personality—both on drums and in his interaction with the cast, crew, and other musicians—brought a very upbeat flavor to the proceedings. Purdie's appearance in the orchestra pit seemed to bring on smiles and teasing all around; he loved it. This was a Broadway show, and you couldn't get more downtown than that unless you were playing under Leonard Bernstein's baton. The play ran at the ANTA Playhouse (now the Virginia Theatre) on West 52nd Street for only forty-eight days. If not a commercial success, it was an artistic one, earning three Tony Awards for Best Actress, Best Featured Actor, and Best Director.

LET THE DRUMS SPEAK!

Purdie was a man of rhythmic ideas. He was always thinking. He adopted a match grip on his drum sticks with both palms down instead of left palm up and right palm down, the traditional grip for a military snare drum slung from the hip in a march. When snare drums went to stands, the awkward traditional grip didn't make any sense yet remained the orthodox technique for decades afterward. Purdie thought for himself and adopted the grip that made sense to him, even if it defied the convention of the time. He even played the butt of the left stick to compensate for his weaker left hand and then learned to feather it with his fingers so that he had power and delicacy in the same stroke, a contrast in sound that would come to define funk drumming. He called it "like hand." Purdie also reversed the conventional positions of his mounted toms to simplify sticking sequences.

Purdie's musical sensibilities were deeply rooted in the contemporary popular music of his generation. He had mastered thousands of contemporary songs and arrangements, which he could summon up effortlessly and then improvise on with ease. Purdie had that perfect balance between playing a part strictly as written and improvising variations that raised the music beyond the imagination of the composer. When that happened (and Purdie tried to make it happen on every piece), the other musicians either got on the train he was driving or were run over by it. Indeed, Purdie purposefully pulled the rhythm section into the groove he was feeling. Once they were unified, he would reach out for the other instruments, often incorporating rhythmic figures they were playing and then adjusting them in the drum rhythm. If the other player wasn't too self-absorbed and listened to what was going on around him, he fell into the groove, and the piece would start to cook like a bubbling stew. Of course, Purdie held the chef's spoon.

In other words, he assumed the role of a conductor. As Leonard Bernstein so eloquently described,

"The conductor is a kind of sculptor whose element is time instead of marble; and in sculpting it, he must have a superior sense of proportion and relationship. He must judge the largest rhythms, the whole phraseology of the work. He must conquer the form of the piece, not only in the sense of the form as a mold, but form in its deepest sense, knowing and controlling where the music relaxes, where it begins to accumulate tension, where the greatest tension is reached, where it must ease up to gather strength for the next lap, where it unloads that strength." − L. Bernstein, The Joy of Music, Simon & Schuster (1959)

Purdie had mastered an impressive variety of styles: big band, jazz, be-bop, Latin, reggae/calypso, theatrical, blues, country, rhythm and blues, gospel—all with that unmistakeable Purdie groove. He seemed to always have a unique twist in anything he played.

Back in Elkton, Purdie had experimented with a unique form of the shuffle—a bread-and-butter pattern figure that is common to the blues, jazz, and some pop music—with a half-time feel driven by hi-hat chirps and delicate partial triplets woven around a very sturdy backbeat. The trains that would shimmy through Elkton at full speed on their runs between New York and Washington inspired this variation. Purdie would emulate the sound, tapping his fingers on the batter head of the snare drum. He showed it to Mr. Heywood, who encouraged him to refine it. Purdie explored the possibilities of the figure until he shaped it to his liking. The Purdie shuffle was born, but it would be decades before it would be accepted.

Even after Purdie had barged in on the "Just One Look" demo session, schmoozing at the clubs would only get him so far. From the time Bill Bivens had introduced him to King Curtis, Purdie was determined to make Curtis sit up and take notice; he wasn't going to leave Curtis alone until Curtis gave him his shot at Small's. Every night Curtis and his band were at Small's, and there was Purdie, sitting at the bar nursing his Shirley Temples and giving Curtis "the look." Curtis ignored him. Weeks passed. Finally, when Purdie least expected it, Curtis called him to sit in on drums. Purdie remembers.

"Small's was a dance club. It was a knockdown, shake 'em up club. I mean, you had to have a smokin' band to play in that club. When Curtis finally said, 'Yes, Come on!' I jumped up, came down, and was getting ready to sit down at the drum. As I was putting my leg across Curtis, started calls for 'Sister Sadie.' Curtis counts off 'One, two' at a super fast tempo. All I did was get my leg down. By the time I got my leg down he was already into the tune and so the only thing that I could do was hit cymbals, you know, I'm hitting cymbals. I haven't sat down yet. I hadn't sat down and wasn't able to adjust the seat or adjust anything. When I finally got a chance to sit down 32 bars later, he said, 'You got it.' Everybody in the band knew what was going on, and they all walked off the stage. They all walked off the stage. I couldn't find one—I couldn't believe it. I couldn't believe it. All I could do was look at him and get mad. I couldn't say anything because I was supposed to have been ready. I kept telling him I was ready. I kept telling him I was ready, you know, 'I can do it. I can do it.' That son of a gun got me. So, when I fumbled and stumbled and fell on my face and—you name it—I did it wrong, he goes back to the top of the song and the song's over. Curtis says, 'Thank you.' I had to get up. I was so upset that I could have killed. I said, 'I'll be ready next time that you play. I *can do it. And I will be ready when you ask me again. And eventually you're going to ask me again because I'm going to worry you to death.' There was nothing that I could say that night. The damage was done. I didn't stay around. I was totally humiliated. I was so upset, I cried all the way home. I had blown my shot. And now I got to figure out a way to get another one. I had to tell myself, 'You'll be back. You'll be back every night that he's there.'"*

Purdie would indeed redeem himself with Curtis, but not that night.

6.

RHUBARB RED

With the success of "Just One Look," Purdie's fortune as a studio drummer began to improve: he started getting more calls to play on demo sessions. After Herb Abramson's partners, Ahmet Ertegun and Jerry Wexler, bought him out of his ownership interest in Atlantic Records, Abramson opened A-1 Studios in Manhattan and became a major client for Purdie. Purdie recorded hundreds of demos for Abramson. Some were released. Many were not.

But Purdie's reputation as a drummer who could make the difference between a hit record and a flop was beginning to take hold among producers, artists, and even arrangers. Of course, Purdie never missed an opportunity for self-promotion. He was a natural leader in these sessions and spoke out about his conception of how a composition should be interpreted. In this way, he would take on the role of an unofficial conductor. Initially, the other session musicians would dismiss Purdie's outspokeness by saying, "That's just Purdie!"—particularly when Purdie put his foot in his mouth. But Purdie was seldom off the mark in his musical judgment, and most producers, including Abramson, valued the extra musical ingredients Purdie brought to the sessions. He seemed to bring a youthful vitality into the studio that was infectious. He joked and kidded, but he never played around when it was time to work. He was always on time. Purdie had a way of bringing cohesiveness into the sessions, whichcarried over into the performance. Nevertheless, Purdie was still young and naïve and on occasion a more seasoned musician would take him aside to school him on the finer points of session protocol.

Purdie was receiving an increasing number of calls for demo work. In his recording studio rounds, he met guitarist Les Paul; the two of them hit it off. In addition to being a legendary recording star even then, Les Paul was also a technical genius. He had invented the solid-body electric guitar, an instrument that made the sound of rock and roll possible. He was also responsible for many recording innovations, including overdubbing and multitracking. Paul recognized in Purdie an opportunity to extend the range of these innovations.

Purdie recognized that overdubbing and multitracking would give him the ability to do what Herb Lovelle said he couldn't—be in two places at one time. The profit motive places a high premium on giving the listening public today the same thing it was willing to purchase in large numbers over the last month, or, better still, the last year. The companies will support a new innovative talent from time to time, but their steady profits depend upon musical recipes that are tried and true. So, when a guitar sound or a drumming style seems to hit the public's fancy, the record producers jump all over it. They ask the musician on their session to sound like "so and so," if the producer can't actually get "so and so" for the session. If "so and so" is booked for another session and can't make it, the producer has a second chance. He can bring "so and so" into the studio at a later time and sweeten the recording. "Sweetening" is a euphemism for producer-managed overdubbing after the session, and with multitracking it can range from adding a track to replacing the original musician on the recording with "so and so" or perhaps a whole new band of "so and so's." Purdie was about to become one of the biggest "so and so's" in the industry.

When Purdie came to New York, four-track recording was the norm. But it wasn't long before four tracks became eight, and eight became twelve, briefly, and then on to sixteen, with no end in sight. Drums have a voracious appetite for recording tracks. Every other instrument gets one track, but drums can use nine, even twelve, tracks, because each drum is miked separately, with some drums taking up two mikes. The hi-hat is miked separately, and the cymbals are miked as a group or separately, depending on how the musician, recording engineer, or producer prefers it.

The truth of the matter is that a trap drum set is not really one instrument. Each drum and each cymbal are individual instruments. In a symphony orchestra, there is usually one musician for each instrument in the percussion section, which includes the crash cymbal, bass drum, snare drum, and timpani, whereas the trap set is a collection of percussion instruments combined into a "contraption" to be played by a single musician. It is a uniquely American musical instrument. One of the skills a trap drummer must master is the ability to integrate the disparate sounds, pitches, and timbres of the set so that its voices emerge as that of a single instrument. This demands an exquisite touch that the musician adjusts to the response of the drum or cymbal being played. If the balance between touch and attack is lost, the sound of the instrument becomes muddled and, worse still, jarring. Anyone can strike a well-tuned drum once and sound fine. It's the second stroke that tells the tale. If you haven't developed touch, the second stroke won't sound like the first, and what follows will sound even more erratic as kinetic energy builds in the stick. Yet if you can control the nuances of the sounds of drums and cymbals, what emerges is a subtle dynamic, an undercurrent that flows just below the volume of the louder drumbeats, which the listener feels more than hears. Purdie was a master at playing this undercurrent, this flow of rhythm inside the rhythm being played. It is like playing counterpoint, except that the second rhythmic line is not parallel to the first, but it is literally contained within the first at a much lower volume.

But at that time, recording technology was quite limited. Reproducing drumming subtleties was often hit-or-miss—most often miss. Purdie became acutely aware that he needed to be knowledgeable about the miking and muffling of his drums during recording sessions. He also had to take into account the mixing down of the session, a process that could result in some instruments being put so far in the aural background that they were barely noticeable to the listener. Purdie could not ignore the recording engineer if he wanted to control his own sound. The engineer and the producer would be in the studio turning the recording dials long after Purdie and the other musicians had left. If Purdie was going to get his full sound on the recording the way he wanted it, he was going to have to learn the technical side of recording, and he couldn't have asked for a better teacher than Les Paul.

Twenty-five years Purdie's senior and born and raised in Waukesha, Wisconson, Les Paul was a sophisticated musician, though he never lost his cornpone manner. He was a real original with a remarkable career. A child prodigy in both music and electronics, Paul performed professionally before he was ten years old, amplifying his own voice and guitar with homemade equipment cobbled together with radio parts. He made his mark as a country singer called "Rhubarb Red," but when he reached Chicago, he fell in love with jazz. So Paul began to live a double life. During the day, he was the country radio performer Rhubarb Red, and by night he was jazz guitarist Les Paul.

In the jazz scene, Paul held his own with the likes of Art Tatum, Roy Eldridge, and Louis Armstrong. After a few years, he dropped his Rhubarb Red persona entirely, formed a trio, and took it to New York, where he performed on national radio broadcasts with Fred Waring. Then Paul went to California and led a house band for such major Hollywood entertainers as Jack Benny, Bing Crosby, Dinah Shore, and the Andrews Sisters. He recorded with Nat "King" Cole on the classic album <u>Jazz at the Philharmonic</u>.

At the same time, he was able to build his now-famous solid-body electric guitar and his own state-of-the-art recording studio, where he invented and perfected recording techniques, such as echo delay, phase shifting, sound-on-sound, overdubbing, and multitrack recording, that are standard in recording studios today. Paul and his talented wife, Mary Ford, made their mark on popular music in the early 1950s with such hits as "How High the Moon," "Tennessee Waltz," "Vaya Con Dios," and "Mockin' Bird Hill." These recordings were made with heavy reverb and multitracked vocals and guitars that took recorded music beyond fidelity to live performance and into a realm of new sounds created by the recording technology itself.

It was in Paul's recording studio at his home in Mahwah, New Jersey, that Purdie did many of his overdub sessions. Purdie recalls,

"Les Paul was working for Atlantic Records in the '60s. He actually is the one who invented multitracking. In my naiveness, I didn't know any of this. All I knew was I would go to his house to work on fixing recordings that he had already put some guitar down on, some bass down on, and some vocals, and then I would just go in and put down drums. Most of the ones that I fixed I had to do the drums over. The drums were so far down in the mix they used that it was hard to even recognize that there were drums. So that's where the multitracking came in. I was playing drums, and he was mixing it from two-track to another two-track machine. So the drums started to become bigger and better and <u>phatter</u>. When I finished, it was like a finished product, but Les Paul would put another guitar thing in or he might put another vocal thing in and they would just go from two-track back to two-track, two-track to two-track. Eventually, he came up with a four-track machine. So Les Paul is the one who invented this, and he's the one who made it successful because he made hit records with it."

LET THE DRUMS SPEAK!

Paul coached Purdie on the musical approach for successful overdubbing. Purdie was used to guiding the feel of a performance by conducting through his playing. But in overdubbing, the performances of the other musicians are fixed. There was no one in the session for Purdie to conduct. Paul didn't want Purdie to merely play along with the recording; he wanted Purdie to breathe life into the musical raw material that was there. Purdie would have to adjust the flow of his playing continuously in the overdub to balance out the time fluctuations he sensed in the guitar and bass. Purdie remembers,

"I would go in, and sometimes there were drums already on the recording, but usually they were so far back in the mix, I mean, they really didn't do anything for the recording. But what was there was the time, even though the time usually fluctuated because of the bass and the guitar being such a dominant factor. Now, Les Paul showed me how to weave a pulse through the flow of the existing tracks and bend it. I did just that through the feel of my eighth notes and my sixteenths, and because I was able to lay back with my left hand. Sometimes it came down to my backbeat or my locomotion in keeping the rhythm feeling like it was moving forward all the time. Well, that was my gift that I've had of playing any music because I was always thinking in terms of the rhythm, the melody,

and the vocal. So, it was just a way of life for me. I actually listened to the pulse of the bass or the guitar or the keyboard. There's always a pulse with any kind of music that you have, I don't care what it is, even when you speed up and slow down, there is still a pulse. A pulse is a feeling like breathing. The music has to breathe. That's the thing where Mr. Heywood told me that's where my gift lies. I could always get into the pulse of what was there because I was always listening. I listen to the whole concept of the music. Each piece of music is a concept, no matter what it is—country, rock-and-roll, or blues."

7.

SOUTH AFRICAN CONNECTION

One of the most enduring musical relationships to emerge for Purdie during his early years in New York was with Galt MacDermot. MacDermot arrived in New York in 1964 from his native Canada on the heels of the hit recording by Julian "Cannonball" Adderley of MacDermot's composition "African Waltz."

How MacDermot got to New York is as fascinating a story as what happened after he arrived. MacDermot was the son of a Canadian diplomat in Montreal, Canada. Under the spell of Nat "King" Cole and Duke Ellington, he took up the piano at age fourteen, after less auspicious beginnings on the recorder and the violin.

In 1950 the MacDermot family moved to Cape Town, South Africa, where MacDermot the elder had been appointed High Commissioner to South Africa by the Canadian government. Galt, by now a confessed jazz head, embraced the music of black South Africa and searched Cape Town diligently to learn more about it. He traveled north into the black mining camps to learn the work songs of the miners. Galt was particularly drawn to the rhythms of

African drumming. The family cook schooled him in the art of African drumming and introduced him to fresh approaches to stock rhythmic phrases. "It's serious music. They're not faking anything," Galt said, reflecting on what he referred to as his "African experience." The ferment of his immersion in African music and culture distilled in Galt a unique musical imagination.

One of MacDermot's earliest compositions from this period was "African Waltz." Years later, the composition was performed in England, where it was a modest hit, but in 1961 Cannonball Adderley's version became a significant hit in the American market, and MacDermot was awarded a Grammy for the composition. Hoping to build on his newly found success, MacDermot left Canada and moved to New York.

After arriving in New York City, he set about recording his own compositions on his own label, Kilmarnock. He talked to a record producer, Rick Shorter, who specialized in assembling studio musicians to record songs for music publishers. One of the musicians Shorter recommended to MacDermot was Bernard Purdie. MacDermot auditioned Purdie and recognized the African beats he loved in Purdie's Elizabethtown beats. It was love at first listen.

Galt's son Vincent MacDermot was just a boy then, but he recalls,

"Dad would record and then he would come home to listen to the tapes, and he'd shut the living room, and we couldn't bother him. And after a few hours, he would let us come in, you know, and then he would point out what Bernard was doing. He'd say, 'Listen to bass drum here,' or 'Listen to what Bernard's doing with the hi-hat,' and I got to appreciate all of the things that he does, you know, because, rhythmically, I mean, he's extremely sophisticated, and my father is too, you know, so they get along extremely well."

Vincent grew up to become a fine musician himself. In fact, the MacDermot family is a musical ensemble unto itself that performs at home for their own enjoyment. Vincent's mother and older sister play clarinet. His twin sisters play flute. His younger sister plays alto saxophone, and Vincent plays trombone. If they had gone on the road, they probably would have compared favorably with the von Trapp family of an earlier generation. The MacDermot children all but adopted Purdie into their family.

Galt MacDermot is also a prolific composer. It is said that Duke Ellington kept his orchestra performing, even when it was losing money, because he wanted to hear his compositions played as soon as they were on paper. MacDermot took the same approach by maintaining a rhythm section of bass, drums, and guitar to back him up on piano in demo-style recording sessions that he would produce himself. Many of these early recordings were stored in his basement and edited for release in several volumes titled <u>The Basement Tapes</u> on Kilmarnock. The bare orchestration on these recordings open a window into the early Purdie style that laid down the foundations of funk drumming.

The bond between Purdie and MacDermot was rooted in their mutual love for percussion. What MacDermot had adopted through his "African Experience," Purdie had inherited from musical roots that penetrated his very soul. Philosophers have probed the mystery of rhythm in music for generations. Even Friedrich Nietzsche wrote on the subject.[5] Although we tend to divide musical elements into categories of melody, harmony, and rhythm, at its most fundamental level, all music consists of patterns of rhythm. Musical notes are vibrations that, when played in a series, constitute melodic lines and, when layered over one another, constitute harmonies, all of which must be played within a broader rhythmic framework of measures structured by time signatures that only partially capture the flow of an actual musical performance. In other words, it's all rhythm. Western music tends to tilt toward the harmonics of rhythm, whileAfrican music leans heavily on its percussive aspects. But the modern American realignment of these musical elements has created a mixture that is downright incendiary. After all, what does Ludwig van Beethoven have in common with Louis Armstrong or Johann Sebastian Bach with Little Richard? How often do these names even appear in the same sentence? Perhaps not often enough. But in the ledger lines of jazz and popular music, they stand cheek to jowl. It's a subject that only an ethnomusicologist could love. In Western cultures the drum is little more than a noisemaker, and the drummer as a "real" musician is suspect. "In Africa it is a drum and not a scepter which is the symbol of the king and the voice of the ancestors." J. M. Chernoff, <u>African Rhythm and African Sensibility</u> (University of Chicago Press, 1979).

Indeed, the first album MacDermot worked on after arriving in New York is titled <u>Shapes of Rhythm,</u> recorded with what Galt dubbed his "Mid-Manhattan Rhythm Section"—Bernard Purdie on drums, Jimmy Lewis (another King Curtis band member) on bass, and "Snag" Napoleon Allan on rhythm guitar. All of this might have seemed unremarkable, but for three weeks in 1967, when MacDermott scored a musical written by two unemployed actors titled <u>Hair</u>. The rest, as they say, is history. After a rocky start, <u>Hair</u> went on to become a musical franchise. "African Waltz" had made Galt MacDermot successful. <u>Hair</u> made him successful, famous, and wealthy. He could write his own ticket, and he did. He plowed his good fortune back into his musical enterprise, expanding his output on his Kilmarnock label, scoring a legion of musicals and film scores, and organizing his own ensemble, The New Pulse Band, of which Purdie has been a member since its inception in 1979. The New Pulse Band[6] performs and records constantly, and over the past twenty-five years, MacDermot has released more than fifteen albums with his ensemble.

But Bernard Purdie didn't do <u>Hair</u> on Broadway. That job fell to Idris Muhammad. In 1967 Bernard "Pretty" Purdie's career blew up. That year Aretha Franklin moved to Atlantic Records, and Purdie was in the middle of it. Aretha Franklin was about to become to soul music what Louis Armstrong was to jazz. It was a defining moment in the history of American music.

Purdie's career had been growing on a number of fronts. He was now doing television commercials, major recording dates, movie soundtracks, live shows at the Apollo Theater in Harlem and the Paramount Theater in Brooklyn, and club performances with his own bands. He was now the number one drummer with King Curtis and the Kingpins (the in-house band for Atlantic Records), and on the weekends he played as a guest drummer with dance bands around New York. Purdie would make cameo appearances, play on a few numbers, and then move on to another venue the same night, where he would play with a different orchestra. Although Purdie was recording primarily in the soul genre, he was also in demand to play with artists performing in a dizzying array of musical styles. That special "Pretty" Purdie flavor seemed to be in demand everywhere.

8.

DEMO KING

Just as Joe Robinson had predicted, Purdie's rise as a session player started with his work on demos. Despite Purdie's fiasco at Small's, King Curtis brought some recording work his way. Purdie also did quite a bit of work for record producer Herb Abramson at his Manhattan A-1 recording studio. (Abramson, acofounder and the former president of Atlantic Records, was squeezed out of Atlantic after his three-year leave from Atlantic during the Korean War.) Through his work for Abramson and King Curtis, Purdie began to gain exposure to the Who's Who of rhythm and blues. He became close to Lloyd Price and Chuck Jackson, both alumni of Sylvia's Blue Morocco, and he recorded with the prolific songwriter and recording artist Don Covay. Covay's breakthrough hit single, "Mercy Mercy," was a significant feather in Purdie's cap. (Jimi Hendrix played on the 1964 recording session of the follow-up album.) An even more significant hit demo-turned-master recorded at A-1, "High Heel Sneakers," by Tommy Tucker, turned out to be Abramson's biggest hit as an independent record producer.

LET THE DRUMS SPEAK!

In 1963 Motown opened its first office outside Detroit under the name Jobete Music, a music publishing company owned by Berry Gordy and his ex-wife Raynoma. Raynoma opened Motown's New York office in the last bastion of Tin Pan Alley, the Brill Building[7] at 1619 Broadway. During this period, Raynoma began an association with record producer Eddie Singleton (they would later marry), who introduced her to his studio band. As a result, Eric Gale, Bernard Purdie, Jimmy Tyrell, Richard Tee, and arranger Bert DeCoteaux participated in all of Jobete's New York sessions. Billy Butler, Carl Lynch and Albert Winston were also very much involved. It is estimated that more than five hundred demos were produced in these sessions. The Jobete office was closed in 1966 after a dispute between Berry and Raynoma. (Little is known about the fate of these demos, although the session musicians suspected they found their way into the Motown catalogue after some sweetening by the Funk Brothers back in Detroit.)

Purdie was steadily developing working relationships with a number of key music arrangers with very strong credentials and huge credibility on the New York recording scene. Horace Ott (The Shirelles' "Tonight's the Night," Nina Simone, Shirley Bassey) was on the "Just One Look" session. Purdie began to work with arranger Sammy Lowe,[8] the pride of Birmingham, Alabama, who arranged and composed for the Erskine Hawkins big swing band for more than twenty-two years. Lowe's career spanned both the swing and the rhythm and blues eras. Lowe was the conductor and arranger for James Brown's recording sessions and brought Purdie in on a number of them; Brown's million-selling single "This Is a Man's World" was recorded in 1966 with Purdie on drums. Purdie also worked with Bert Keyes, the pianist for Ruth Brown and a noted R&B arranger with Rama Records. George Kerr was another arranger of note with whom Purdie began to work during this time.

The musical chemistry of the rhythm section is critical in any recording session, but on demo sessions, where the essential ingredients are the artists and the rhythm section, that chemistry is the whole ball game. In the broadest sense, the entire ensemble is one big rhythm section, but on a demo it's bass, drums, keyboards, and guitar. The bass and drums capture the heartbeat of the music by expressing the pulse (not to be confused with the tempo) of a composition.[9] That pulse is carried into the harmonic structure by the piano and guitar, where it shapes the interpretation of the piece by the entire ensemble. The musical personalities in the rhythm section are the factors that make for a tight unit; that's why music producers sometimes use different drummers, bass players, guitarists, and other instrumentalists on different compositions performed by the same artist on a single CD or album. Steely Dan made a career out of shuttling session players in and out of their recording sessions.[10] Of course, some musicians will have a more diverse musical palette to draw from. Purdie was one of these twice-blessed musical stylists. He was comfortable in any style, from theatrical pit work to the funkiest "get-down-with-the-get-down" roadhouse blowing, from big bands to be-bop, from country and western to Latin percussion at the Paramount theater in Brooklyn, Purdie could do it all flawlessly.

"Mr. Heywood taught me very early in my life never limit yourself to one kind of playing; you go with the flow of the music. That's the way I was taught. Yeah! Now, I didn't know I was playing rock, jazz, blues, funk, soul, country, hillbilly, New Orleans, march music. It was just music to me. And I know it's—I know it's hard to explain, but to me it was strictly, strictly music. I have never put a category on music, except music. I like all kinds of music, so why can't I play it? That's what I've always said, because I can see it. It's all about a concept. That's how I was taught. Everything is a concept. The notes are not going to change. The only thing that changes is the rhythm, and if you understand the rhythm of the music, you can play it. A quarter note is a quarter note, eighth note is an eighth note, a sixteenth is always going to be a sixteenth, but how you interpret it is where the rhythms come in. It's all a concept. That's why when I forced the Purdie Shuffle on people, it took years for them to understand what I was doing, all the little subtle things

that never got in the way, and, consequently, that is what kept motivating people and moving people. It's a movement—feel. They could feel it, but they didn't know what it was. And nobody else was doing it, so they kept coming back to me. That's why so many demos that I made became hit records. Now, they tried to re-create records, and they couldn't do it; the other drummers couldn't do it, so they put the record out, and they were hits. "High Heel Sneakers" was a hit, "Mercy, Mercy" by Don Covay was a hit. (I never got paid the $15. Through today I refuse to accept the money from him because this means that he would be in my debt for life. We became friends. We really became friends and even close to almost [like] family members, but I refused to take the money from him, so he would always be in my debt.)" – Bernard Purdie

Producers develop relationships with certain session players whose judgment they trust to select the other players on the session. These contracting musicians will usually play on the session. The contracting musician is paid more, but more importantly, the contracting musician accumulates a reservoir of goodwill with the session players he brings to the job. For the record producer it usually means getting the best session players for the date. It is an incentive to get the contracting musician on the date with other players he's compatible with. Conflicting schedules are a real problem in getting in-demand session players on a date, but these players will go out of their way to accommodate the contracting musician, because he is a source of future work.

Over time certain combinations of musicians tend to develop a demand for their collective musical sound. Purdie found himself a part of a particular recording unit consisting of Richard Tee on piano, Eric Gale on guitar, and Jimmy Tyrell on bass. Later, Chuck Rainey and Jerry Jemmott would work with Purdie extensively. Although keyboard and guitar are part of the rhythm section, its core comprises the drum and bass. Ideally, the whole rhythm section is tight, but as Purdie would put it, there has to be a love affair between the drums and the bass.

In 1964 Raynoma Mayberry Liles Gordy and Eddie Singleton found themselves in jail for bootlegging the Motown hit "My Guy" by Mary Wells. Raynoma accepted an offer of settlement from Berry, the Jobete office in New York was closed, and Berry and Singleton were released. After his release, Singleton made Purdie an offer he couldn't refuse, even though it would take him away from the New York recording studios: a two-week engagement in the Bahamas. Purdie stayed for six months. He was captivated. He took up with local musicians, who gave him a place to stay. He was having a ball. Purdie played six days a week with local groups at the big hotels in Nassau, where he was a superstar and treated like one.

Purdie's musical reputation wasn't confined to the Bahamas. Word spread quickly to Jamaica, where a young singer named Bob Marley was recording a new sound called reggae. Through the influence of expatriate [11]American record producer Arthur Jenkins, Purdie found himself in Kingston, recording with Bob Marley and the Wailers. Jenkins was looking for a crossover sound, so Purdie played on the first three Marley albums, even as he was learning how to play in a reggae percussion ensemble. This experience would prove indispensible in his later excursions into Latin music. Purdie remembers Marley as a very peaceful and introspective man who took his time in the studio to get his music right. Johnny Nash was another rising reggae vocal star with whom Purdie recorded; it was Nash's brother who brought Purdie to Jamaica in the first place. One track that Purdie recorded with Nash—"I Can See Clearly Now"—would become a huge hit in the United States. New York was very far away, and, like Ulysses, he was under a spell that kept his mind far from home, but eventually the call of New York became too strong to resist. The spell was broken. Purdie went home. He was as thin as a rail.

Six months is an eternity in the life of a session player. When you leave the scene, you are quickly forgotten. Purdie's return to New York City was not met with a ticker-tape parade. Nevertheless, Purdie was ready to get down to business, determined to make up for lost time and to break into the major recording sessions. It finally dawned on him that Abramson was using the demo sessions as final productions and getting away with paying his musicians peanuts. But, as Purdie would later say, "When you don't know, you don't know."

Purdie decided to go on the offensive and take control of his situation. He would engage in an exercise known in the marketing world as product differentiation. He would become a brand name. He labeled himself Bernard "Pretty" Purdie, the hit-maker. That decided, he went about doing something so unorthodox that it is still talked about to this day: he made miniature billboards to advertise himself in the studio during sessions. It was Jimmy Tyrell who really came up with the idea and suggested it to Purdie, who quickly embraced it. Across the street from Purdie's home was a sign-making shop. Purdie told the owner what he was trying to do, and the owner made three signs in a size that he could mount on a music stand. One sign read "The Little Old Hit-Maker, 'Pretty' Purdie."[12] The signs were adorned with color graphics designed by the sign shop owner, who was so enamored with the idea he didn't charge Purdie for the work. From then on even if producers didn't remember Purdie's name, they could say, "Get the kid with the signs!" It was a stroke of genius. Some musicians hated him for it, but Purdie was not one bound by convention. He played the music business like he played the drums— aggressively. Soon Purdie had more demo work than he could handle.

9.

BOOGALOO BUGSY

Argentina gave the world the tango. Brazil gave birth to the samba. The Dominican Republic lays claim to the merengue. But the great engines of Latin music in North America are Cuba and Puerto Rico. Cuba has provided the musical forms growing out of its native dance, the <u>son</u> (the rumba, the mambo, and salsa are derivations of the <u>son</u>). Puerto Rico has cultivated what we now call Latin music in the United States, particularly after Fidel Castro came to power in Cuba and the United States severed economic and cultural ties with the island. The steady influx of Puerto Ricans and expatriate Cubanos into New York City has maintained the critical mass necessary to keep the music alive and evolving in the United States.

Latin music is inseparable from Latin dance. The musical forms are African, and the style of music invariably takes its name from the dance style it accompanies. The idea that music is performed in a concert with the audience sitting and quietly listening is completely foreign to this musical tradition. African-based music demands participation. You must at least tap your foot, bob your head, clap your hands, or, best of all, dance, dance, dance. It is a form in which the musicians and the audience perform together.[13] These African musical roots are close to the surface in Latin music.

In the mid 1960s a number of Latin bandleaders in New York consciously sought to record Latin music with an R&B flavor. Joe Cuba and Johnny Pacheco were early proponents of the style, which came to be known as Boogaloo. What this musical concept required to make it work was an R&B trap drummer who could adjust to the feel of Latin percussion. Trap drummers didn't ordinarily play within a percussion ensemble (Dizzy Gillespie's be-bop collaboration with *conguero* Chano Pozo notwithstanding), and traditional Latin percussion ensembles don't normally include trap drums. Simply adding a trap drum to the ensemble doesn't mean the sounds are going to blend. The Latin music bandleaders and record producers needed the right trap drummer to make the concept work commercially.

Fania Records was to Latin music what Atlantic Records was to soul music. Johnny Pacheco, a Julliard-trained Latin music artist from a musical Dominican family and a former New York City police-officer-turned-lawyer named Jerry Masucci founded the label. Masucci was neither Hispanic nor a musician, but he fell in love with Latin music while studying business administration at the University of Havana and working for the Cuban Tourist Bureau.

Legend has it that one day, Pacheco met Masucci at his law office to consult on a legal matter and hit the lawyer up for $3,000 to start his own record company. Masucci put up the money, the two men shook hands on the deal, and in 1964, Fania Records was born. Masucci was to handle the business end and Pacheco was to produce the music. Fania opened an office at 56th and Broadway and grew quickly. One of the first artists to sign with the new label was pianist Larry Harlow, later of <u>El Judío Maravilloso</u> (the marvelous Jew) fame:

"Fania started about '65. I was the first artist with Fania. It was me and Pacheco, and it kind of built up from that, but Fania always wanted to make that crossover into the American music scene. There was a period in the late sixties, when there was a movement called the Boogaloo that was going on in New York. Joe Cuba, Joe Bataan, and Johnny Colon came out with the boogaloo material at about the same time. It was really like bang-bang, push-push, Joe Cuba kind of stuff but with English lyrics. They figured [that] by having English lyrics, it would get play on American radio stations.

We never used trap drums in Latin music. We used timbales. So we were always looking for a drummer who, first of all, could read, and who had the feel that could blend in and mix that boogaloo-shingaling. Latin drummers alone couldn't play that. The Spanish guys couldn't bastardize the cowbell. They were very straight. They were purists, Cuban purists. So, we turned to the African American guys, because those were the only guys who could really get down, you know. Bernard had that thing. I always loved Bernard's playing. Bernard wound up on a couple of those boogaloo-shingaling sessions with all the guys, and they just kicked ass all over the place. But Bernard played—I think he played—on the Joe Bataan recordings. I think he played on Ralfi Pagan recordings, you know, "I Want to Make It with You." I'm trying to think of all the old guys that sang in English—Oh, God, Johnny Colón, maybe Willie Colón." – Larry Harlow

Marty Sheller, a Grammy Award–winning New York composer and arranger for Fania and later with Columbia Records, remembers:

"For those who needed an American drummer to play along with the Latin rhythm section, Bernard was the man. A lot of the times, they did sessions that required that special feeling in the rhythm section, and they would call Bernard. And every opportunity I had in doing any projects where they gave me the leeway to say this is who I would like to use, he was always the first choice. In that era, he was really the man. Of all the drummers that I can think of he was the best one to play that kind of thing, and I don't recall them

using too many other guys to work on their projects. He was always the first call. And, as a matter of fact, I remember that there were sometimes [when], if he were not available, they would kind of postpone the date to try to get it when he would be available.

He has terrific technique but he's not a flashy drummer in the sense of 'look at how great my technique is.' It is all used for the purpose of getting the groove right. Staying in that pocket. All of his energies are focused on that. The thing that most impressed me about him was his musicianship, his ability to adapt to the material and really make it happen. But when you're playing with a Latin rhythm section you've got a timbale player, you got a conga player, and maybe even a bongo player as well, along with the traps. So, there's so much happening there that the trap drummer has to really be aware of all of that so as to still establish the groove but not get in the way. That's what impressed me so much about him. He had very big ears, listening to what's happening and knowing what to do to make it happen."

The boogaloo era at Fania Records was an intense but brief period that peaked in 1969. Latin-soul was controversial among the Latin music purists who saw it as a compromise rather than an evolution. Fania went on to bury boogaloo under a new wave of more traditional Latin music marketed by Fania as salsa. Johnny Pacheco

("The Maestro") went on to earn nine Grammy nominations over a stellar career that continues today. In 1997 Jerry Masucci died at his residence in Buenos Aires at the age of sixty-two, leaving an estate estimated at over $300,000,000.

But Latin funk did not end in 1969. It continued well into the 1970s, led by Cuban-born <u>conguero</u> Mongo Santamaría. "Mongo" means "chief of the tribe," and Santamaría believed his family tree led back to the country of Mali, on the western edge of the Sahara Desert. Santamaría's mother wanted him to play the violin, but the voice of the drum was much stronger in the boy who was born in the Jesús María barrio of Havana. As Mongo's later recording anthology title suggested, it was the power of "Skin on Skin." His professional start came in the 1940s, at Havana's legendary Tropicana Nightclub, a must-see venue for well-heeled tourists and business travelers to Cuba in the pre-Castro days.

Santamaría came to the United States in 1950 with the original "Mambo King" Pérez Prado, [14]followed by stints with Tito Puente and Dave Brubeck alumnus Cal Tjader. In the late 1950s, Santamaría took the plunge as a bandleader and never looked back. His first Latin soul hit was the very unlikely "Watermelon Man," written by the genius composer/pianist Herbie Hancock, who was then a member of arguably the strongest jazz quintet ever, the second Miles Davis Quintet.[15] In a feat that only Pérez Prado had ever accomplished, Santamaría visited the pop charts a second time in 1969, with his interpretation of the Temptations' hit "Cloud Nine." The recording is practically a drum battle between Santamaría and Purdie. Marty Sheller recalls the 1969 Columbia Records recording session.

"The session was terrific. American drummers usually play with a laid-back kind of feeling, which is great for funk, you know. The kind of things that Bernard would tend to play were a little more right on the beat, which is why he had such a crisp kind of energetic kind of sound. And in Latin bands it's very much right on the beat. Mongo's experience, and my experience as well, with American musicians who have not had the opportunity to play with Latin bands, is that they tend to lag behind the beat. Bernard was right on it. So, when they started playing together it was an immediate—like you could even see it in the eyes; they were smiling at each other because they both recognized that they were right on the same page. So, it was a real pleasure to have someone there that could fit right into the style of what Mongo was doing, and they really hit it off."

Santamaría became a legend in his own right. He had both the talent and the charisma to bridge the gulf between the Hispanic and the gringo musical cultures. When Santamaría and Purdie played together, it was truly a rhythmic contest of two giants going at it hand to "like hand."[16]

10.

PHILADELPHIA STORY

"But Bill, we can't do any better than that!"

Although Purdie is identified with Atlantic Records because of his relationships with King Curtis and Aretha Franklin, he never signed on as a staff musician with Atlantic, despite being offered a position. Many musicians might become frustrated with the hustle of moving from studio to studio on different jobs, but Purdie loved it. Besides, he made more money being an independent session player. He recalls having more than sixty different employers in one year. One of his biggest accounts was Columbia Records, and one of the reasons for the size of the account was Columbia producer Billy Jackson.

Billy Jackson was a black wunderkind. He had a wonderful singing voice, and he was smart, ambitious, and willing to work tirelessly to make something of himself. After working at a company where he picked jukebox records based on his judgment of their popularity, he got a job with Philadelphia radio and television personality Jerry "The Geater with the Heater" Blavatt (Philadelphia's version of New York's Alan "Moondoggie" Freed), where he displayed a real talent for producing Blavatt's shows.

Jackson was also a member of The Tymes, a Philadelphia singing group that made a record called "People." "People" was produced by Tommy Bell, one of the principals at Philadelphia International Records, a label that under Kenny Gamble and Leon Huff eventually would rival Motown Records. Jimmy Wisner, a brilliant pianist and a Philadelphian as well, took the record to Columbia in New York. A deal was struck. Columbia promoted The Tymes, who went on to have a string of hits, the most well-known of which was "So In Love." Wisner went to work under Clive Davis at Columbia as its West Coast vice president, and Wisner hired Jackson for Columbia's East Coast A&R staff on the strength of Jackson's production of a very successful Blavatt show featuring the then-new group Sly and the Family Stone and their new record "Dance to the Music." "Dance to the Music" became a hit, and Sly and the Family Stone became a national sensation.

When Jackson started working in New York in the mid 1960s, he was shocked to find that very few of the session players on recording dates were black. He was secure enough to go to the main session contractor in New York City and tell him that he would not use him unless he started seeing some black musicians in the sessions. After all, Columbia Records was a 500-pound gorilla in the industry.[17] Then Jackson approached Purdie to pull together a session band. Purdie pulled in Ralph McDonald (percussion),

Richard Tee (keyboard), Paul Griffin (keyboard), Eric Gale (guitar), and Chuck Rainey (bass). They became Jackson's primary session band. A good contractor has to be efficient. His musicians must be reliable and show up on time. They must be able to read and yet play with the right feel. Purdie started renting drums to be set up in different locations so he could just show up at the session, record, and then move on. A contract musician who puts it all together is paid double and sometimes even triple scale.

As Jackson recalls,

Yeah, we're talking about the early sixties, and Purdie was always the layman's drummer because Purdie was accepted by producers to play on any kind of music. Purdie's greatest asset, I think, at that time, was that he could read. It wasn't because they wanted him, it was because Purdie could read. Now, Purdie's personality came out in whatever they gave him, because Purdie was also a heavy drummer. He wanted you to know that he was on the record; he wanted you to know that he was there on the date. So, you always got a little extra when you had Purdie. You know what I mean? Purdie would play what was on the charts, but he would give it that extra little thing and put his personality and everything he had into the music, and that impressed me. That really, really impressed me. . . . And Purdie's the only one that can actually do what I wanted done. *A lot of musicians were caught up into who they were and their schooling, and they had only the ability to read and not actually read and feel. And Purdie was the guy [who], if you came in and you said to Purdie, 'I need this kind of ...,' he'd say, 'Oh, I know what you want,' before you could get the words out of your mouth."*

But sometimes Purdie's band was too efficient. Billy Jackson remembers:

"Oh, I have another great story about Purdie. I did a song that became a huge hit. I had Purdie, Ralph McDonald, Chuck Rainey came in from LA, and Eric Gale, and they were all charging me triple scale. Me, the guy who was helping them. I came in to record 'If You Let Me Make Love to You Why Can't I Touch You' by Ronnie Dyson, for Columbia. This was around 1969–71. We go into the studio, and Purdie says to everybody, 'Okay, we all know what we got to do. I got somewhere to go.' He puts up his signs and everything else and then says, 'Okay, look, I got to be out of here.' And, of course, everybody says—because this is what they did— 'Yeah, Purdie, do your thing.' And Purdie would his thing. Purdie would say, 'This is Bernard 'Pretty' Purdie playing the drums.' And he would hit his sticks for everybody to pay attention, and no sooner than the drum hit, it was like magic. I swear it was like magic. And

then Purdie says, 'Okay, that's it!' Now, I'm the guy that's supposed to say, 'That's it!' I'm paying the bills and representing Columbia. So I turned to Purdie and all the guys, and I said, 'I can't pay you three times what you're worth and you come in and do one take. I can't justify that.' And you know what they turned around to me and said? I'll never forget this. All of them turned around and said, 'Hey, Bill, we can't do no better than that.' And sure enough it was the truth."

But the guys would reciprocate,

"If I ever called them for a date, they came. I remember one time when I had some clams casino. I was in the studio, and I had big stage set up. Purdie was my contractor, and we had a band of forty people. You ever had a bad clam? I hope you never do. But it was the first time that there was elimination in every part of my body at the same time—including my eyes. Purdie and the guys came in and found me on the bathroom floor of the studio, and Purdie says, 'Don't worry, Bill. We'll finish the date. Don't worry about it. Go home.' I was out of it, totally. And they finished my session. So, Purdie and I got to be real tight. And, you know, when Purdie and his guys went to triple scale, all of the other musicians got jealous, and they wanted to get paid if you went a minute over. But that never happened with Purdie's band."

Purdie had a long musical relationship with Columbia Records, especially A&R director, producer, songwriter, and arranger Jimmy Wisner who had many pop hit records.

The 45 rpm single was still the king format in the 1960s; to every producer, record company, and artist, a hit record was one that would be in demand as a single. Long-playing albums were secondary and wouldn't come into their own until the 1970s; before that the decision to issue an album was made after the singles were released. Typically, a single recording session was organized to put down the "A" track and three or four other tracks, one of which was to be selected as the "B" side. The unreleased tracks might later be used as material for a long-playing album, which also would include the tracks previously released on the single. Producers wanted to get everything right on the "A" side of the single, so they spent most of the recording time on that side, giving the "B" sides much less attention. The session players, therefore, got more creative freedom on the "B" sides. Ironically, the "B" side became the hit more often than one might imagine. An overproduced recording was as much a mistake as an underproduced one. The key was getting the right balance. The best producers knew how to achieve the balance between the musical discipline of the score and the creative instincts of the instrumentalists, particularly the rhythm section.

The recording industry dropped the label "race records" in the late 1940s in favor of "rhythm and blues," a term coined by Atlantic record producer Jerry Wexler when a journalist with <u>Billboard Magazine</u>. But race did continue to matter to the recording industry of the 1960s and well after that. Crossover records (records that were hits on both the pop charts and the R&B charts) were still rare. Producers and arrangers were very conscious of what market they were selling to; they turned out pop records to appeal to predominantly white record buyers and R&B recordings for black customers. Motown was an exception in that it aggressively sought a musical formula for black artists that would give them crossover appeal to the much larger and more affluent pop market. Atlantic Records prided itself on producing black artists to bring out their inherent talent on the theory that good music will always be in demand, whatever the audience.

As with most of the black instrumentalists brought into recording sessions behind pop artists, Purdie was sought out because the producer and arranger wanted an R&B feel in the recording. If an R&B feel wasn't needed, Purdie wasn't called—or, if there was a mix of tracks, some with an R&B feel and some pure pop, a white drummer and a black one might be on the same session. In general, recording professionals assumed that black musicians weren't disciplined readers, an assumption seemingly based on the idea that black musicians were poor or slow readers, which only reinforced the bias favoring white session players for calls to record. On the other hand, producers looked to black instrumentalists for solo improvisations with that special feel that they brought to their instruments. In any case, white players got the ensemble work and black musicians were brought in as ethnic specialists to put the "roux in the gumbo,"[18] so to speak.

Purdie recalls one recording session at the huge Columbia Studio on 30th Street. The session involved a very large orchestral ensemble. Purdie had been called in to play on some of the tracks, while a white drummer was to play on others. The producer wanted a soulful, funky, rhythmic feel on Purdie's tracks, and he wanted the white drummer to play the subtle shadings of the written score on the other. After a lunch break the white drummer was a few minutes late getting back to the studio, and the producer had called one of his pieces, unaware of the drummer's absence. Purdie quietly slipped on to the drum throne and sight-read the score with all the shadings the producer wanted—not playing a hint of funk, soul, or R&B. When the white drummer got back to the studio, Purdie had already secured his spot, replacing him for the session. It was a case of "When you move, you lose!" Purdie, determined to break the old stereotypes, looked for any opportunity to prove that he was a complete musician, proficient in more than one musical genre.

Grammy Award–winning producer Jimmy Wisner recalls.

"I'm a member of the Grammy organization, and my wife and I go frequently to the Grammy affairs. We went to one of the marquee theaters [in New York] fifteen years ago, and Purdie was in the house orchestra that night. I was absolutely amazed, because that was the night where there were so many different styles of music, and we always associated Bernard Purdie with R&B. But the ability he showed to play so many different styles that night—and so well—was just incredible. I think that's a tribute to him."

Purdie's apprenticeship with Mr. Heywood and the Clyde Bessicks Orchestra gave him a musical dimension that set him apart. He knew how to move a big band in precise written arrangements, in a style that was both contemporary and tasteful. Purdie brought a soulful sensibility to big band arrangements, and as big band arrangers and producers became more familiar with his capabilities, they began to hire him for recording sessions and live performances. Guitarist Don Costa was the widely known conductor and arranger for Frank Sinatra in the 1960s and 1970s. He was the master of the big band arrangement and worked extensively with Eydie Gorme and Steve Lawrence as well. What is much less well known is the extent to which Costa used Purdie to play his studio arrangements, conducting a series of sessions in Chicago with Purdie because he couldn't find a Chicago drummer who could give him the performance he wanted. Purdie was on the short list of big band drummers used by Jimmy Wisner, Johnny Pate, Chicho Wilshire, Burt Keyes, Burt Decatotis, Horace Ott, Apollo Theater arranger Al Sears, Herb Bernstein, Joe Renzetti, Artie Butler, and Hamilton Granville, among others. Supremely gifted musicians, these arrangers could orchestrate compositions for large ensembles and then put an orchestra through its paces in the studio, while making creative adjustments on the spot. Purdie really admired the talents of these arrangers, and he learned a great deal from them.

Purdie recalls one such session with Chico Wilshire. Wilshire had written an orchestral arrangement that included a drum part. Using some of Purdie's signature drum licks, he had written the drum portion with Purdie in mind. When playing the piece, Purdie started "adjusting" the arrangement. Wilshire stopped recording and instructed Purdie to play the part as written. Purdie was headstrong and continued to insert his own improvisations. Whilshire stopped again. This went on for an hour with the meter running, until Purdie finally played the whole piece as written. Wilshire then turned to

Purdie and said, "Okay, now play it the way you want to." Purdie learned to respect the fact that when an arranger makes the effort to create an arrangement, he should hear his own arrangement at least one time as written, before the drummer changes it. Purdie loved Wilshire for his patience in dealing with a young, headstrong drummer, but as Purdie is often fond of reminding you, "I was never wrong about the music." The released version was the Purdie version.

Jimmy Wisner realized that Purdie's contribution to a session went well beyond his ability to play the drums.

"Purdie has always had a tremendous understanding of what records were about. It's not enough to be a good drummer or whatever you play; you have to have a sense of what the needs of a recording are. And it's different. They're not the same. There's a quality about Purdie that really is infectious in a positive way. And joyfulness is the way to describe it."

Purdie has a pulse—a feel—in his playing that is infectious. He has an attitude that says to his bandmates, "I'm coming through, and if you're not with me, get out of the way." His playing is insistent. This is the quality that most arrangers wanted from Purdie and wanted on their records.[19]

BERNARD PURDIE

Horace Ott used Purdie whenever possible.

"Whatever I was doing, first call was Bernard. I mean, there was no question about it. It meant that I could concentrate on other things because I didn't have to worry about what he was going to play, because I knew it would be right. Bernard would be looking around, and he's checking the other guys out. His number is—Bam! Bam!—right there. You can hang your hat on it. I'm sure most arrangers and conductors felt that way. You didn't have to worry about Bernard. He was a metronome. First of all, you didn't have to worry about the beat going somewhere. And you also didn't have to worry whether the groove was working. It just automatically happened.

Bernard was great at handling the complexities of an arrangement. We're at letter A, then letter B, then reverse to the chorus. We're in the fade. We're in intro. You get to bar 27 and it's very similar to bar 38, but it's not the same. You didn't have to worry about Bernard. He would just make it happen. Bernard's not bashful, and he would make sure the other guys were paying attention. He'd say, "Look at this. Okay, now let's try it." When you find guys that work together like that, that was the goodness of it all. People would reschedule a session if Bernard couldn't make it."

11.

CHICAGO SOUL

The Jazz Age was a tale of three cities: New Orleans, Chicago, and New York. New Orleans gave birth to jazz, but jazz came of age in Chicago and New York. When jazz spawned R&B in the early 1950s, New Orleans was its midwife, but New York was the capital of the record industry, leaving Chicago a second city in popular music. Eventually Los Angeles overtook Chicago, as its huge entertainment industry propelled it into a shooting war with the East Coast over competing claims of hip-hop supremacy. The music powerhouse of the Midwest became Motown, which was founded in Detroit. It seemed that Chicago would forever remain in musical short pants. Yet Chicago had too much native talent and creative energy not to give it a voice at home. Chess Records gave voice to the Chicago blues scene, and Brunswick Records gave voice to Chicago Soul. Jackie Wilson, Jerry Butler, The Chi-Lites, Curtis Mayfield, and The Impressions all recorded on Brunswick. With the death of Jackie Wilson and the taint of a payola scandal, the promising label would collapse. But in the 1960s and early 1970s, Chicago's Brunswick Records was riding high.

BERNARD PURDIE

Independent producer Carl Davis was Chicago's answer to Berry Gordy, producing at various times Jackie Wilson, The Chi-Lites, Gene "Duke of Earl" Chandler, and a host of other Windy City artists on the Brunswick label. Davis had worked as an A&R man for Columbia Records for a time, and perhaps this is how he became familiar with Purdie's work. In any case, Bernard recorded Jackie Wilson's biggest hit "(Your Love Keeps Lifting Me) Higher and Higher." He also recorded "Have You Seen Her" by the Chi-Lites and "Turn Back the Hands of Time" by Tyrone Davis. These were the biggest hits, respectively, of each of these artists. Davis also made use of the famous Funk Brothers, the Motown house band, who would slip out of Detroit on the weekends to moonlight in Chicago. Whatever their contribution to Motown's success, the Funk Brothers weren't in the same league as New York studio musicians. They operated within the confines of the very narrow, albeit very successful, Motown musical formula—one that wasn't very portable or as demanding as the variety of material that Purdie had mastered. There was one hitmaker in the 1960s and 1970s: Bernard Purdie. As New York jazz producer Bob Porter put it,

"Purdie was an innovator in the sense that he is the essential soul drummer of the 1960s, and what he brought to it has carried on since then. Forget Benny Benjamin at Motown. Purdie was a much better drummer all around. Purdie was not only a guy who could

read and could cut charts, he brought just everything that you would want to a session, and he worked sometimes three, four sessions in a day, working with a variety of people. Purdie really built the sound of soul music and New York-based soul music in the late '60s."

12.

THE JAZZ MASTER

Purdie's dominance in R&B did nothing to diminish his presence on the jazz scene. Because of the heroin epidemic that continued to ravage its community of musicians, he downplayed any strong association with the jazz world. Nonetheless, he loved jazz music and enjoyed performing it. Once producers and artists pigeonhole a musician as jazz, orchestral, R&B, Latin, rock, pop, or country, the label becomes a prison. Purdie took any work he could get, but his feel, his ability to sight-read, and his musical instincts in organizing session ensembles made him valuable in a number of different genres and presented him with opportunities to extend his reputation as a marquee player in several categories of music.

Purdie's musical relationships were spreading in many different directions. Ironically, his earliest documented sessions on major recordings were in jazz, not R&B. There's nothing unusual about jazz drummers being called upon to record R&B tracks, but it is very unusual that any musician would have his feet planted in both worlds simultaneously for any extended period. And the journey is usually from jazz to R&B, not the other way around. But by the end of 1967, Purdie had played on jazz albums released on Prestige,

Verve, and Blue Note— legendary jazz labels that documented the artistry of the most sophisticated jazz virtuosos in music history.

"Pretty" Purdie recorded with the likes of the great composer/saxophonist Benny Golson for Verve and the great composer/pianist Horace Silver for Blue Note. These were very serious musicians who had a great deal to say about who played on their albums. The great producer Bob Porter didn't do rock or R&B. But there was something in Purdie's playing that transcended genre. He heard it, and he wanted some of it. Funk drumming was being fused with jazz in much the same way that it was being fused with Latin music; the common denominator seemed to be Purdie's version of swing, called "The Groove."[20] Again, it is a style that looks to percussive rhythm to inspire the harmonic and melodic lines of the improvisation that lies at the heart of jazz.

One of the best examples of this is the recording of a live performance of Dizzy Gillespie at the 1980 Montreux Jazz Festival. Playing behind Gillespie were jazz harpist Toots Thielemans on guitar and Purdie on drums. No bass. This stripped-down jazz ensemble highlights the interaction of Purdie on the drums and the improvised melodic lines of Gillespie on trumpet. Thielemans is almost lost in the mix, but his sparse, harmonic lines hold the performance together.

Purdie's musical presence on the jazz scene brought him to the attention of legendary jazz producer Bob Thiele. Thiele, a prodigy who had hosted his own jazz radio program, owned his own record label and edited Jazz Magazine before he had turned eighteen. He had written the memorable "What a Wonderful World" (reintroduced to the public by Louis Armstrong on the soundtrack of the movie Sleepless in Seattle). He discovered and promoted the great Buddy Holly. He produced A Love Supreme by John Coltrane, arguably the most influential modern jazz performance ever recorded, and helped launch Jackie Wilson's career. Thiele worked with everyone from Lawrence Welk and Henry Mancini to Teresa Brewer, whom he later married. He was as eclectic as Purdie was versatile.

Thiele had his own label, Flying Dutchman, but he was largely an independent producer who worked with major labels such as Decca and RCA Impulse. He saw in Pretty Purdie an opportunity to extend his considerable reach, so he offered Purdie a place in his office suite on the ninth floor of 1841 Broadway. Purdie jumped at the chance of working with Thiele; he dreamed of producing himself, and, in fact, had assumed the producer's role in many of the sessions he played on. As a contract musician, he was one step closer to his goal.

The list of performers Thiele had produced was impressive, to say the least: Coleman Hawkins, Sonny Rolands, Oliver Nelson, Quincy Jones, Count Basie, Coleman Hawkins, Duke Ellington, Louis Armstrong, etc. It was a Who's Who of jazz and popular music, with a little rock and R&B thrown in for good measure. Thiele had his fingers in so many different musical pies that Purdie was left to his own initiative, producing many of the sessions he played on, although Thiele was credited as the producer. Purdie didn't understand the importance of being attributed as a co-producer; he was just happy to have the opportunity to do the work and to learn. In the course of his apprenticeship, Purdie produced sessions with Louis Armstrong, Oliver Nelson, Eddie "Cleanhead" Vincent, Gato Barbieri, Leon Thomas, and Gil-Scott Heron. Purdie even produced a record of his own under the name "Pretty Purdie and the Playboys," titled <u>Stand by Me—What You See Is What You Get</u>. The Louis Armstrong sessions produced a tribute album to the great trumpeter, titled Louis Armstrong and His Friends, on the occasion of his seventieth birthday; that album includes the Bob Thiel classic "What a Wonderful World." Purdie played drums and co-produced it.

13.

MR. BIG SHOT

Purdie doesn't recall exactly when it happened, but at some point, his career just exploded. Columbia Records, Atlantic Records, RCA, and Capitol Records were beating a path to his door. It wasn't just the major record companies that sought him out; he had started with independent record producers and small record labels, and they wanted him even more. It seemed that every producer in town saw Purdie's sound as an essential ingredient for a hit record, regardless of the style of music. He was playing and recording rhythm & blues, jazz, dance bands, be-bop, theater, movie scores, commercials, and even Latin music. It was a dizzying array of assignments, and Purdie revelled in his busyness. He could no longer operate out of his home. He needed a business office and a secretary. He went out and got both.

Purdie was also woodshedding (a musician's term for practicing alone) so that he could keep up the pace and play anything with anyone at any time. He had long since redeemed himself with King Curtis. Determined to erase the memory of that awful night that Curtis had ambushed him on the bandstand, Purdie had gone into training for a rematch. It probably hadn't been neccesary, as far as

Curtis was concerned. By now Curtis knew what Purdie could do. But Bernard had wanted the world to know he wouldn't shrink from a challenge. He had practiced "Sister Sadie" until he could handle it at any tempo, even standing on his head.

Then he had marched back to Small's and taken his place at the bar, Shirley Temple in hand. When Curtis called him up, Purdie was ready. Purdie recalls,

"Curtis called 'Sister Sadie' again. I got in, I sat down. This time I had a minute to sit down. So, he had counted off, bam, right to the tempo. I went right into it. And then Curtis says, 'You got it.' And when he said that I went right to the funk, cut the tempo all the way down to like a fourth of what the tempo was and started playing the funk. I came out of the funk, moved into the 6/8, from the 6/8 to the Latin, and from the Latin I started building myself up, doubling, and building up until I came all the way back to where the tempo was. I was now back up to my tempo, and the band kicks back in and I'm saying to myself 'You can play. You've done good.' Curtis came over and he smiled at me."[21]

The year 1965 started off auspiciously for Purdie. By that time, he was playing behind King Curtis regularly. Curtis's drummer, Ray Lucas, was getting attractive offers to go on the road with Dionne Warwick, who was riding a string of hits composed by Burt

Bacharach. The Bacharach compositions broke all the rules for popular success. The songs had odd meters and clever phrasing, but Warwick made them accessible to the most casual listener. They were enormously popular. Bacharach and Warwick had a formula that neither artist was going to tamper with. Purdie was subbing in the Kingpins more frequently, as Lucas went on the road. Weary of life on the road, Belton Evans, another regular with Curtis, left the Kingpins entirely. It wasn't long before Purdie was the band's number-one drummer. By early 1965 Purdie was firmly entrenched, so when King Curtis opened for the historic[22] Beatles concert at Shea Stadium on August 15, 1965, Bernard "Pretty" Purdie was on the drum throne before 55,600 Beatles fans and 2,000 police officers. Purdie knew he had finally arrived.

Purdie opened an office in midtown Manhattan with bassist Jimmy Tyrell and sent for his oldest brother, Henry, to come from Elkton to manage his bands. Purdie still had the New York unit he had put together during his time at the Comet Club. Now that Purdie had some musical clout, he brought the band from Baltimore up to New York and put them up at his home on 113th Drive. Purdie managed go-go girls and singers as well, and it was Henry's job to keep them all busy.

Purdie had so much work at that point that his life consisted of running from one job to the next —from an Alan Freed show at the Paramount Theater in Brooklyn to the Apollo Theater in Harlem to a recording studio in Manhattan to a club in the Bronx to play with one of his bands to a Long Island affair as a guest drummer with one of the New York area dance bands. His secretary kept track of his engagements and Henry made sure to keep his stable of musicians busy with club dates. Purdie tried to bring the club band from Baltimore into the studio, but the weak reading skills of the musicians really hampered them. They did some studio work, but they remained essentially club musicians and gradually drifted back to Baltimore. Meanwhile, Purdie was traveling in increasingly diverse musical company. He was establishing musical relationships with Dizzy Gillespie on one side of the musical spectrum and James Brown on the other.

Purdie also worked a bizarre job in 1965 that landed him another number-one record. He was called in to record behind an obscure teenage garage band from Dayton, Ohio. The record producer said that he wanted the drum sound of an imaginary inexperienced thirteen-year-old drummer playing in his first teenage music group. Purdie had too much musical pride for that but not enough to turn the job down. Angry about it, he decided to play so immaturely that the producer would be forced to abandon his idea. The producer didn't. The record was released and went to number one on the record charts.

The group was The McCoys, and the song was "Hang On Sloopy," composed by Wes Farrell and Bert Russell (Bert Berns), who also produced the record. The record not only hit number one, but in the 1965 college football season the Ohio State University Buckeye fans adopted it as their theme song. It remains so to this day, in part, due to the foresight of the OSU marching band that broke with its conservative musical tradition and went with playful spirit of the piece, putting a special arrangement of it in the band's repertoire. In 1969 the 166th General Assembly of the State of Ohio proclaimed "Hang On Sloopy" the official state rock and roll song.[23] No other state in the union has an official rock and roll song.

PART III
TURNING POINT

14.

ATLANTIC RECORDS

Atlantic Records, the result of an unlikely partnership between the son of a Turkish diplomat and a Jewish dental student, was destined to showcase to the world the music of black America wrought with the astute musical and business judgment it deserved. But first, the Ottoman Empire collapsed. Ahmet Ertegun was born into a privileged family in his native Turkey. In the wake of World War I and after the fall of the Ottoman Empire, Turkish society was modernized under the rule of Ataturk; by government decree, the Munir family became the Ertegun family. Ahmet's father, Munir Ertegun, served as Turkish ambassador to France and then to the United States during World War II. Consequently, the Ertegun siblings grew up children of privilege in the Turkish embassy in Washington, D.C. Ahmet's mother, Hayrunnisa, was a great lover of popular music and was very musical herself. Ahmet and his older brother, Nesuhi, inherited her love of music and, in particular, they were captivated by jazz. Before arriving in the United States, they envisioned it a "land of cowboys, Indians, Chicago gangsters, beautiful, brown-skinned women, and jazz."[24] But such adventures would have to wait while they endured the less romantic lives of prep school students.

Even so, their love of jazz never waned, and as they matured in the environment of racially segregated Washington, D.C., the reality of those barriers forged in them empathy for the artists who had created the exciting music they loved so much. Ahmet and Nesuhi began to use the Turkish embassy as a musical sanctuary for renegade jazz performances, inviting mixed-race jazz ensembles to perform at private jam sessions in the embassy. Ahmet was even arrested with three of his college classmates leaving a black nightclub in Annapolis, but the authorities were not about to prosecute the children of prominent families, much less the son of the Turkish ambassador, so no charges were brought. Occasionally, Ambassador Ertegun would receive a letter from an outraged Southern senator about the "goings-on" at the Turkish embassy, to which he would reply, "In my home, friends enter by the front door; however, we can arrange for you to enter from the back."[25]

Soon Ahmet and Nesuhi were promoting integrated jazz concerts in Washington, D.C., at the Jewish Community Center and the National Press Club Auditorium; they featured Sidney Bechet, Big Joe Turner, Lead Belly, Teddy Wilson, Zutty Singleton, and J. C.

Higginbotham, among others. They were now rubbing elbows with the likes of Duke Ellington, Lena Horn, Johnny Hodges, Lester Young, and Jelly Roll Morton.

Ambassador Ertegun died shortly before the end of World War II. His body was interred at Arlington National Cemetery until the war ended. President Harry Truman honored the ambassador's memory by having his body returned to Turkey in-state aboard the USS Missouri, the battleship on which the Japanese surrender had taken place several months earlier. The ambassador's body was received in the Port of Istanbul by thousands of his countrymen, who festooned the docks with flowers in celebration of his return.

If it had not been for the fall of the Ottoman Empire, Ahmet and Nesuhi Ertegun would have had no choice but to return to Turkey after the ambassador's death, in order to complete their studies and eventually become lawyers or diplomats, as was traditional in their family. As it was, they were given a choice of returning to Turkey with their family or remaining in the United States to support themselves as best they could. But there would be no more chauffeured cars, servants, or cooks. They decided to stay, and their decision would change history in the recording industry in the United States.

Nesuhi headed to California to pursue his interest in the origins of jazz and the blues. He managed his wife's Jazzman Record Shop in Los Angeles and taught courses in jazz and folk music at UCLA. Ahmet, on the other hand, was determined to start his own record label. He felt that he knew black life and black music in America, as well as the roots of black American music in the gospel and the blues. He cared deeply about black music and the musicians who performed it, but he knew little about the record business, and he had no money. He had never worked a day in his life, and after his family returned to Turkey, was left with a small stipend while he studied for his master's degree at Georgetown University.

Ahmet was so broke that he had to sell his beloved record collection just to get by. Undeterred, he went looking for investors and a business partner. He became a partner with his friend, Herb Abramson, a New York University dental student who worked part time at National Records as head of A&R (artists and repertoire). But Abramson had no money, either. Ahmet convinced Lionel Hampton to back his venture, but Hampton's wife, who handled her husband's money, quashed the deal. He went to family and friends for money but got nowhere. Finally, Ertegun convinced his own dentist to invest $10,000 in his company. Ertegun and Abramson named the label Atlantic (because every other name they could think of was taken) and set up an office in a condemned

Manhattan hotel called The Jefferson, just off Broadway. Ertegun slept in a hotel bedroom and ran Atlantic from his living room. It was late 1947, and the American Federation of Musicians had called a nationwide recording strike to begin on January 1,1948.

Despite these inauspicious beginnings, over the next fifteen years, Atlantic Records prospered and grew to become the envy of every independent record company in the country; Ahmet Ertegun became a very wealthy man. Ertegun recorded music he liked. It wasn't pure jazz, and it wasn't the blues. It was the beginnings of rhythm and blues: Ruth Brown, Ray Charles, the Drifters, La Verne Baker, Clyde McPhatter, The Coasters, Don Covay, Bobby Darin, Ben E. King, Solomon Burke, Hank Crawford, Wilson Pickett, Sam and Dave, the Young Rascals, Otis Redding, Percy Sledge, and Aretha Franklin, among others.

Herb Abramson was called back into the Army for the Korean War and Ahmet brought in Jerry Wexler, then a journalist with <u>Billboard Magazine</u>, as a partner. Wexler had coined the term "rhythm and blues" at <u>Billboard,</u> when he convinced the publication to drop the term "race records" as a music category. Wexler, like Ertegun, was not a musician but came into the business as an avid record collector and a devotee of black music. He turned out to be a gifted producer, as well.

In 1955 Ahmet convinced Nesuhi to produce jazz recordings for Atlantic. The result was that John Coltrane, Ornette Coleman, Charlie Mingus, the Modern Jazz Quartet, Roberta Flack, Lee Konitz, Bobby Short, Phineas Newborn, Milt Jackson (with Coleman Hawkins, with Cannonball Adderley), David "Fathead" Newman, Mel Torme, John Lewis, Mose Allison, Stephane Grappelli, Herbie Mann, Sonny Stitt, Art Farmer, Nat Adderley, Max Roach, Carmen McRae, Eddie Harris, Elvin Jones, Allen Ginsberg, Joe Zawinul, Charles Lloyd, Freddie Hubbard, Chick Corea, and Shelly Manne, among others, recorded on Atlantic. The label's association with black music in the 1950s and early 1960s resulted in its signing a number of popular "British invasion" groups of the late 1960s and 1970s. Atlantic was the heavyweight champion of independent record companies until 1967, when the entertainment conglomerate Time Warner acquired it. Ahmet Ertegun remained at the helm, but Jerry Wexler chafed at the corporate bridle. He departed in the early 1970s, but not before he had one last big musical fling, a world-beater at that: a shy gospel singer from Detroit named Aretha Franklin.

15.

ARETHA FRANKLIN

By 1967 Bernard Purdie was the buzz of the recording world, and his schedule was completely out of control. The New Yorker is the height of literary sophistication in magazine publishing circles; it prides itself on its coverage of the New York art scene. In its November 18, 1967, issue it covered the Purdie phenomenon in a piece titled "Pretty Purdie." The article followed a day in the life of Purdie, from his advertising jingle for the Benton & Bowles agency in the morning, through his recording session with the Shirelles in the afternoon, to his evening session with James Brown. It describes Purdie's day as a delightful hustle from one job to the next; eating on the run; and laughing, joking, and cajoling musicians, producers, engineers, and artists into seeing things the Purdie way. It was a glimpse of the Purdie personality in full effect.

The year 1967 was big for Atlantic Records as well. In February Atlantic co-owner and producer Jerry Wexler signed Aretha Franklin to the label. Franklin had been under contract with Columbia Records, who had produced her as a jazz singer. When her Columbia contract expired, she jumped to Atlantic. Wexler was not himself a musician, but as a producer, he had an instinct for matching an artist with the right material and the right session players and then working the session environment to bring out the fullest potential of the mix. With Aretha Franklin he had a lot to work with. As Purdie described it, Franklin's music was as much in her fingers as in her voice. Wexler put her at the piano for the early Atlantic sessions, and then his ear led him to produce Franklin with an all-white rhythm section in the small northeast Alabama town of Muscle Shoals. The studio musicians included Chip Moman, lead guitar; Jimmy Johnson, guitar; Spooner Oldham, electric piano and organ; Tommy Cogbill, bass; and Charlie Chalmers, Ken Laxton, David Hood, and Joe Arnold on horns. A fight broke out between one of the session musicians and Franklin's husband, so after only one completed track ("I've Never Loved a Man") and a partial second track ("Do Right Woman, Do Right Man"), Wexler brought the whole boxing match back to Atlantic's recording studio in New York, where King Curtis got involved. What resulted from the Muscle Shoals/New York sessions was some of the most soulful music ever to hit planet Earth. The first two tracks were released as the A and B sides of a single: "I Never Loved a Man" and "Do Right Woman, Do Right Man." Both sides were hits. The single went to number 9 on the pop charts, but as time would tell, this ranking didn't even begin to measure the true strength of her music.

Why Wexler had not gone with Curtis and his band in the first place is unclear. But when the session migrated to New York, with the Muscle Shoals musicians in tow, Wexler stayed with Roger Hawkins on drums behind Franklin in the studio. Despite his current association with Franklin in the public mind, Purdie is not given credit on any of the immensely popular early Atlantic sessions from 1967, 1968, and 1969. Indeed, Purdie's name didn't appear on an Aretha Franklin album for nearly five years after she signed with Atlantic Records. The Kingpins performed with Franklin live and on the road. King Curtis and various instrumentalists with the Kingpins are credited on her recordings from the beginning of her association with Atlantic. But the complete absence of Bernard Purdie on any of these recordings for five years is incomprehensible.

Roger Hawkins had that down-home feel in his playing, and perhaps Wexler didn't want to mess with success. After all, Franklin charted top singles with Hawkins holding down the drum chair. Hawkins' work on "Chain of Fools" was the kind of gut-bucket fatback drumming that propelled Franklin's rendition of Don Covay's masterful composition into a new realm of soulfullness. And the deep pocket Hawkins mined in "Respect" was just what Franklin needed to support her interpretation of the late Otis Redding's posthumous hit song, whichshe recorded only two months after his tragic death in a plane crash.

But other drummers had recorded behind Franklin from time to time. Gene Chrisman is credited as the drummer on two cuts on her 1967 monster hit Atlantic album, I Never Loved a Man the Way I Love You—"Dr. Feelgood" and "Soul Serenade." The "Dr. Feelgood" recording is classic Aretha Franklin, while "Soul Serenade" was a hit written by King Curtis that he had recorded years earlier; it was Curtis's theme song. The overwhelming number of Franklin's session dates from 1967 through 1969 were recorded with Hawkins on drums, but Ray Lucas, Al Jackson, Tubby Ziegler, Sammy Creason, and even Bruno Carr, got their shots to record with Aretha Franklin every drummer except Bernard Purdie, who, with Ray Lucas, was the drummer for King Curtis and the Kingpins and who played for her on the road. At this point, Purdie was the most in-demand studio drummer in the business.

Purdie had clashed with Wexler in a non-Franklin session, when Wexler asked him to play like Panama Francis. Purdie would have none of that and told Wexler so in the session. Purdie told Wexler that if he wanted Panama Francis, he should call him for the job. Wexler shut the session down, which was extraordinary, considering the probable expense involved. King Curtis tried to smooth things over, but Wexler must have been unpersuaded.

Curtis was to Purdie in the music business what Leonard Heywood had been to Purdie growing up. A man of great musical gifts and great charisma, King Curtis was Purdie's rabbi and a musician whom Purdie held in the highest esteem. Purdie loved Curtis like an older brother, and there was a great affection between them. Curtis talked to Purdie about the incident with Wexler and chided him for being so direct with him in the session, telling him that he needed to learn to be more diplomatic. Purdie took Curtis's advice to heart, but the damage may have been done. There was no bigger recording sensation than Aretha Franklin in the late 1960s, and Purdie seemed out of the play.

Yet Purdie's reputation didn't suffer during this period. He had more work than he could handle, having been offered a job with Atlantic Records as a salaried staff musician, which Curtis advised him against. "Just look at your income last year and compare it to the salary offer," Curtis told him. Financially, it would be a huge step down. In many instances Purdie was commanding double or even triple union scale. Acting as a contracting musician for an ever-increasing number of record producers gave him tremendous clout. Also, Purdie's musical relationships were spreading in many different directions. He was doing commercials, Broadway shows, hit records, and live shows at upscale venues; he worked with the best producers, arrangers, artists, engineers, and session players in the business. He was practically producing many of the sessions he was playing, selecting the musicians, and directing them in the studio. He worked with large ensembles, and, in one instance, even put together a string session for a performance at the Apollo Theater and conducted the orchestra while another musician played drums.

Purdie was understandably proud of all he had achieved in just five years. But his youthful brashness was degenerating into obnoxious bragging. What the industry accepted as youthful enthusiasm when Purdie was just out of his teens was now considered the mark of a person whose ego was out of control. Perhaps Curtis was too restrained to tell Purdie what his enormous talent and his quick rise in the business had done to his head, but he couldn't bring himself to confront him about it.

Even old Cap, now 104 years old, weighed in. In his gentle way, he told Bernard he should avoid alienating people—the musicians he was working with and such. (Purdie had to look the word "alienating" up in the dictionary.) Purdie frequently visited Cap in Elkton, where he would find the elderly man sitting in that same living room chair that Purdie had slept in for so many years after his mother died. He confided in Cap about his family troubles and his musical triumphs. Cap could see through to that Purdie ego, whichwas both a blessing and a curse on the Purdie men. Purdie respected Cap's wisdom and advice. He tried to change, but it seemed almost programmed into his temperament. Yet gentle persuasion wouldn't do it—Purdie needed something similar to a Herb Lovelle tongue-lashing.

It came completely out of left field. Purdie was attending a social event, at which he was regaling a group of his admirers with stories about his recent projects. A female acquaintance pulled Purdie aside and dressed him down about his incessant self-promotion and, to cap it off, she told him he was using words he didn't really know the meaning of. In other words, he was both loud and wrong. Purdie tried to defend himself, but he was stung. He accepted the rebuke. He would get help with his vocabulary but curbing his habit of self-promotion didn't come easily to him. Purdie was sincere, but he just wasn't humble. Having grown up scrapping for every dime he ever made and every opportunity he was ever given, he had to let the world know about his gift and prove himself in every musical outing. His playing was an outgrowth of his personality. He was ebullient and enthusiastic. He wanted everyone to know the joy he felt when he was playing. But Purdie finally recognized that there was a difference between self-confidence and self-promotion. He resolved to curb the latter as best he could.

Moreover, Purdie harbored ambitions beyond playing drums. He saw himself as a record producer and perhaps a record company executive. He knew that he had the drive, the stamina, and the intelligence to succeed on the business side of the music industry. Purdie wanted to be all that he could be, but such a scattered approach carried risks. His broad musical capacities were often a surprise to many producers who tended to pigeonhole him into a narrow musical category. It was difficult for gifted instrumentalists to branch into other areas without losing their chops. In Purdie's experience, bandleaders tended to be more businesspeople than musicians. Those who succeeded musically and in the music business needed someone behind the scenes who could manage the details of a broader enterprise. Bernard's brother Henry had filled that role, but Henry moved on after a couple of years. Bernard opened an office with bass player Jimmy Tyrell with visions of starting a record label. But two absentee entrepreneurs were no better than one. The call of the studio and the bandstand were too strong for either of them to resist. Regardless of their business potential, they were primarily players at heart.

The musical <u>Hair</u> opened on Broadway in 1968. It was at the height of disaffection with the war in Vietnam, punctuated by the assassinations of Martin Luther King, Jr., and Robert Kennedy just two months apart. <u>Hair</u> was the perfect vehicle through which young people in those times could express themselves. Purdie had recorded the demo soundtrack of <u>Hair</u> with Galt MacDermot, but Idris Muhammad handled the original cast recording and theatrical work. Purdie was too much in demand in the studio to commit to the production. He continued to record with MacDermot, doing <u>A Woman Is Sweeter</u> (Kilmarnock, 1969); <u>Two Gentlemen from Verona</u> (Kilmarnock, 1971), which was Galt's second musical; and the soundtrack of <u>Cotton Comes to Harlem</u> (United Artists, 1970), MacDermot's first film score.

Purdie recorded four albums under his own name during this period: <u>Soul Drums</u> (Date, 1967), which he produced; <u>Soul Fingers</u> (Camden, 1968); <u>Stand By Me/Whatcha See Is Whatcha Get</u> (Mega, 1971); and <u>Purdie Good</u> (Prestige, 1971). In 1967 and 1968 Purdie had recorded more than twenty jazz albums and untold numbers of R&B singles and demos. In 1969 and 1970 Purdie doubled his output. Purdie began to regularly entertain producers, artists, and musicians at his home, where he would prepare barbecue and some of his big-pot Elkton dishes. Aretha Franklin, Roberta Flack, and Donnie Hathaway were just a few of the artists he entertained. Purdie even moved to a larger house to accommodate these parties.

Purdie's freeze-out of the Aretha Franklin recording sessions ended on February 16, 1971, when Jerry Wexler brought together a powerhouse session group to record with Franklin at his Criteria Studios in Miami. With the brilliant Donnie Hathaway on keyboards, Cornell Dupree on guitar, Chuck Rainey on bass, and Purdie on drums, it was clear that Wexler was taking no chances. The result was four tracks, all of which Wexler thought strong enough to release as singles: a remake of Ben E. King's hit "Spanish Harlem" and three Aretha Franklin compositions ("Rock Steady," "Day Dreaming," and "All the King's Horses"). "Rock Steady," a rhythmic indulgence, became for Purdie a signature performance, serving as his "Topsy" and his "Drum Boogie" all in one. Purdie wasn't accompanying Aretha Franklin on the record; rather, <u>she</u> was accompanying <u>him</u>. The Chuck Rainey and Bernard Purdie bass and drum combination would become legendary. Chuck Rainey described it this way:

"Bernard played with a full nuance. You could hear all the inside of his playing or what they call weak rhythms. You sort of put them in your head when you're playing a mundane figure. If you're playing a certain feel, you hear all the other rhythms within that.

Bernard plays the dominant rhythm, but he also has a lot of energy in playing the nuances. And he doesn't make them obvious to where I have to play what he's playing. We just play the groove, but I don't have to make the accents. Other drummers are trying to do the same thing, but they make the structure so definite that in order to make it flow I have to agree with the accents that they choose and put them into the rhythm for my own pattern. But with Bernard I have a whole spectrum, as long as I play the groove. That's what separates him. He's got a good feel, but it's not in your face to where you have to play certain things. You just have to play the groove. So, you have a choice. You have a choice of what to play within his groove and that's what makes all the difference."

16.

SPIRIT IN THE DARK

Reverend C. L. Franklin, Aretha Franklin's father, said it best. "Aretha is just a stone singer."[26] She was all that, and more, and she had the gold records to prove it. Although Atlantic had enjoyed six number-one records with Franklin on the R&B singles chart, only Franklin's "Respect" had crossed over to reach number one on the pop charts. Her R&B fan base was huge but capturing a bigger share of the pop market would mean an extraordinary jump in record sales. Efforts to move Franklin into jazz and show tunes to broaden her audience had resulted in disappointing sales. Then Wexler had one of his million-dollar brainstorms. San Francisco's Fillmore West was a unique venue[27] because music promoter Bill Graham had built a following of young mixed audiences that were as open to the music of Rashaan Roland Kirk as to the Rolling Stones or Otis Redding. The audiences were more than just fans of the particular artist. They seemed to bond into a family at the performances regardless of the performer.[28] They were relaxed, hip, and ready to have a good time. Graham cultivated in his events a pioneering musical spirit that eradicated old social barriers of class and color. The core of these audiences was made up of the new beatniks (Wexler called them "longhairs"), who rallied around the music their parents turned their noses up at. It was the psychedelic era, and whilepsychedelic music drew more heavily from the folk tradition than from the blues, both types of music were deeply felt. The audience wanted more than entertainment; they were looking for spiritual uplift. The Fillmore West was too small to accommodate an audience of sufficient size to pay for Franklin's appearance, so Wexler decided to record the concerts to make up the difference.

There are times when everything just comes together in a particular concert. The audience is primed, the artist is on fire, the band is pumped, and the chemistry is perfect. Often those performances are not captured on a recording because no one really knows when they are going to happen. Wexler's instinct in setting up the Fillmore West recording date was inspired. He and Graham scheduled a series of three concerts for Friday, Saturday, and Sunday of the first weekend in March of 1971. Located in a ballroom/recreation center (the dance floor doubled as a basketball court), the Fillmore West was little more than a glorified high school gymnasium situated over a San Francisco car dealership.

But Franklin's artistry was not the product of drawing-room sensibilities. This was authentic, down-home music played with an energy and enthusiasm that came right out of the sanctified church. Wexler didn't want an orchestral backing, which had beenAretha's show band on her earlier live album <u>Aretha in Paris</u> (Atlantic, 1968). To ensure the right feel, Wexler went with the in-house recording unit for Atlantic Records, King Curtis and the Kingpins. The core unit was Curtis on soprano, alto, and tenor saxophones and a rhythm section of Bernard Purdie on drums, Jerry Jemmott on bass, Poncho Morales on congas, and Cornell Dupree on guitar. To his own ensemble Curtis added Billy Preston on organ (a star in his own right), Truman Thomas on piano, and the five-piece The Memphis Horns (Wayne Jackson on trumpet and Andrew Love on tenor saxophone, augmented by Jimmy Mitchell on baritone saxophone, Lou Collins on tenor saxophone, Roger Hopps on trumpet, and Jack Hale on trombone).

Franklin and her background singers, the Sweethearts of Soul (Brenda Bryant, Margaret Branch, and Pat Smith), were from Detroit, but all the musicians, with the exception of Truman Thomas, were southerners. Curtis and Dupree were from Fort Worth, Texas, and Billy Preston was from Houston. Jemmott was from Macon, Georgia. The Memphis Horns hailed from Memphis, and, of course, Purdie was from Maryland. Poncho Morales was from Mississippi. This was the funkiest band imaginable. When the word got out about it, the instrumental musicians from the Bay Area showed up in droves. They weren't disappointed.

LET THE DRUMS SPEAK!

The three-night engagement opened on Friday, March 5, 1971, at a packed Fillmore West. It was a sellout. King Curtis opened the show with a brief introduction of Billy Preston and The Memphis Horns and then counted down an up-tempo rendition of Eddie Floyd and Steve Cropper's "Knock on Wood," a rousing foot-stomper released by Memphis's Stax label in 1966, with Floyd on vocals backed by house band Booker T. and the MG's. It was a showpiece for The Memphis Horns, who had played on the original recording session. Curtis stepped aside and let The Memphis Horns have at it. Purdie kicked it off on the count of four, and The Memphis Horns hit that unforgettable introduction: [29]

Andrew Love jumped on the melody, mimicking Curtis's trademark "yakety sax" style, while Purdie settled into his "locomotion," with hi-hat chirps pushing his backbeat and a perfect touch on his lightning-fast bass drum. At that tempo, consistent, 32nd-note bass drum doubles are almost inconceivable, yet Purdie played them with unerring accuracy and at the perfect volume. Preston had his Hammond B3 locked into Dupree's rhythm guitar licks in a combination that complimented Jemmott's long bass lines. Morales keyed on Purdie's bass drum as a sort of pseudo clave. The groove was irresistible. Love took the first chorus on tenor, with Jackson taking the second on trumpet. They traded choruses until Jackson improvised an extended elaboration of the theme. Then the other horns became more insistent and pulled Jackson back into the horn section to end the performance with a restatement of the introduction. The whole thing was a roiling, boiling soul extravaganza.

The audience went wild with excitement. It didn't need any more warming up, but Curtis wasn't finished. The band launched into two more high-energy numbers. Led Zeppelin's "Whole Lotta Love" was in keeping with the eclectic musical programming that Graham promoted, and Buddy Miles's "Them Changes," recorded by Jimi Hendrix's Band of Gypsies, had become a psychedelic soul anthem. Curtis slowed things down a bit in the middle of his set. Procol Harum's "A Whiter Shade of Pale" was followed by Billy Preston's then-current hit "My Sweet Lord," which finally broke the psychedelic spell and moved the music back to its southern roots with the sad tributes "Ode to Billie Joe" and "Mr. Bojangles." Then Curtis ramped things up with his big hit of 1962, "Soul Serenade." Performing "Memphis Soul Stew," Curtis introduced the Kingpins in turn, as the ingredients of the stew were added one by one into the cooking pot: first, a cup of Jemmott's funky bass, followed by a pound of Purdie's fatback drums and four level spoonfuls of Dupree's Memphis guitar, then a pinch of Billy Preston's organ and another pinch of Memphis Horns, and a dash of Mississippi congetto from Morales, finally, all stirred up with Curtis's tenor sax. Eventually, the stew was bubbling, as the ingredients mixed and mingled in the final chorus. Curtis closed his set with Stevie Wonder's "Signed, Sealed, Delivered (I'm Yours)," which brought the show a little closer geographically to Franklin's hometown. Curtis's ensemble had nearly burned the building down before she ever got on stage.

After intermission, Bill Graham gave one of the shortest introductions in music history. As if to say, "We all know why we've come here tonight," Graham simply announced, "Aretha Franklin!" Up in the house went a cheer of such volume that Curtis had to stomp the tempo by slamming his heel on the stage floor, turning the whole stage into a gigantic metronome. SLAM, SLAM, SLAM, SLAM, and the whole band erupted in unison on the first beat of the measure. It was a furious pace for the rhythm section, as The Memphis Horns blared a fanfare heralding, "The queen is on her throne!" The audience recognized the opening line immediately. It was the ghost of Otis Redding in sixteen bars and the voice of Aretha Franklin in the seventeenth. "What you want / Baby I've got it!" she shouts to her imaginary lover. But she demands something from him—"RESPECT!": one word that spoke volumes about men and women, haves and have-nots, blacks and whites. Only in the spirit of the blues can a sexual innuendo become a rallying cry for universal brotherhood.

Aretha pressed on as the Sweethearts of Soul responded "Whoop!" "Not much, just a little bit!," and, of course, "Sock it to me!," in all the right places. Then Purdie broke the beat down, and the band went from forte to pianissimo instantly. The queen addressed her subjects. "Good evening. Hi. Hello. Welcome to the Fillmore West and to our first and only show tonight. We're going to ask you to do just one thing for us, and that is to relax. Let us use your soul for just a minute. I promise you, before you leave here, you will have thoroughly enjoyed this show as much as you've enjoyed any that you've had occasion to see. All right?"

With that, Aretha changed gears completely, performing a waltz, her own composition titled "Call Me," which Atlantic had released a year earlier on her album <u>This Girl's in Love with You</u>. It was a nice change of pace from the highly energetic "Respect." Next up was a rather complicated arrangement of several complex melodies written by Jimmy Webb ("Up, Up, and Away," "MacArthur Park," and "By the Time I Get to Phoenix"). The arrangement starts with Purdie striking a clanging cymbal, while Preston drifts up and down the keyboard and Jemmott and Dupree pluck their axes in a disconnected manner. There's even a wolf's howl (Purdie himself!) in the mix. It's spooky and totally out of keeping with the show's earlier material. Then, out of musical left field, Purdie explodes with six bars of a fast pick-up line that he repeats six times. It's a countdown, and the rest of the band joins Purdie in tempo to give Aretha a two-bar introduction into the first stanza, "I'll let you go my angel / Though I want you to stay." The lyrics dance through a series of strange harmonic progressions, and then the song suddenly ends as it began, with the clanging cymbal and the wolf's howl bidding the audience farewell. After the song Aretha said, "Kinda way out. Did you like it?" The audience is lukewarm, so the song is dropped from the set list for the following nights. But Aretha, who can do no wrong, proceeds through the middle of her set with songs by Stephen Stills, Paul Simon, Lennon and McCartney, and David Bates of the group Bread. These R&B arrangements of pop tunes have "crossover" written all over them.

The last four songs of the set bring Aretha back home after her pop odyssey. "Don't Play That Song Again" is a 1962 hit by Ben E. King and written by Atlantic founder Ahmet Ertegun and gospel artist Betty Nelson. Ashford and Simpson's "You're All I Need to Get By" is pure R&B. But all this is a buildup to the last two compositions, both penned by Franklin. The first, "Dr. Feelgood," cowritten with her husband, Ted White, came out on her first Atlantic album, I Never Loved a Man the Way I Love You (1967). It's a song so integral to her musical personality that no one dares try to cover it. "Dr. Feelgood" is a funky, sensual blues in three-quarter time that never fails to work up an audience. The lyrics are unsurpassed in their joyful soulfulness. Franklin is completely uninhibited in her rendition of a song about a woman and her social priorities concerning her girlfriends and her man, but Aretha's delivery of "Dr. Feelgood" has a subtle churchiness to it. In fact, she's not just telling the audience about Dr. Feelgood; she's testifying about how he makes her feel. This becomes clearer as she begins to exhort her "congregation" in the manner of a preacher leading a prayer meeting, except now the subject of her sermon changes. "Sometimes I get a little fearful but as sure as the sun rises in the morning, I know that everything is going to be alright. Yeah! Yeah! Yeah!" It's no longer a concert; it's church. She moves seamlessly into "Spirit in the Dark," addressing the audience as she would a congregation of spiritual brothers and sisters. It's pure gospel now, right down to the double-time chorus, when the church sisters show their church steps, a hop on the offbeat (one AND two AND three AND four AND). When she finishes, the audience is yelling, "MORE! MORE! MORE! MORE!" Aretha takes a reprise: "Do you feel it? Yes Lord! Every day I walk with the spirit.

Help me to walk right! Help me to talk right!" Aretha Franklin wasn't just entertaining; she was proselytizing.

On Saturday night King Curtis dropped three numbers from his set. Aretha substituted "Share Your Love with Me" for "Mixed-Up Girl," but her set stayed the same length. She opened with "Respect" and closed with "Dr. Feelgood" and "Spirit in the Dark," with the prayer meeting exhortation in between. As exhilarating as Friday night had been, by Saturday night the whole ensemble had hit stride. The performances were flawless and polished (which may mean that the instrumentals were overdubbed). All the rough edges had been smoothed out. The first instrumentals were runaway soul trains. Jermott was the engine; Billy Preston and Cornell Dupree, the tie rods; and Purdie, the steel wheels keeping the band on the track and in the groove.

After the performances, Purdie held court with the legion of Bay Area drummers who had come to hear and see him play. By this stage of his career, Purdie was greatly revered by aspiring drummers influenced by his session work and his live performances. His reputation outside of New York grew mostly by word of mouth. It wasn't easy to find out who was playing drums on recordings in that era. In the 1960s the whole objective of a recording session was to produce a hit single, and that meant a 45-rpm vinyl disk with no liner notes or attribution to the session players. With the exception of jazz recordings, even long-playing albums didn't identify the session players. But real fans have a way of finding out what they want to know.

One young drummer in the audience was only a year away from becoming a drum legend himself. Recently discharged from the Air Force, David Garibaldi had joined an Oakland band called Tower of Power, which had opened the show. After the show, Garibaldi sought out Purdie, who gave him some words of encouragement. Garibaldi is always quick to acknowledge Purdie's influence on his playing. Two years later, in 1973, that influence showed up in a significant waywith the release of Tower of Power's self-titled fourth album. Garibaldi had achieved a funk-drum feel so tightly integrated into the arrangements that he practically redefined the genre. The whole group performed like a Swiss watch in a deep-funk pocket, without a hint of the technical pretentiousness that infects some performances. To be funky is to be a little ragged, because real life is rough around the edges. That's one of the elements that the blues influence brings to the music: honest, fidelity to what is, no pretense, and always a lot of joy. Tower of Power was completely unique and yet solidly grounded in that Bay Area ethnic confection of soul with a Spanish tinge. Garibaldi would depart the group after a few years, but he would leave a huge footprint on the music scene. In that sense, he and Purdie were kindred musical spirits.

The last night of the engagement at the Fillmore West was pure magic. The 1971 release on Atlantic Records is a superb live recording, but it can't be expected to do justice to what happened on that final night. In 2005 Atlantic released a four-disk set titled <u>Don't Fight the Feeling: Aretha Franklin & King Curtis Live at Fillmore West</u>. It covers all three nights of the performances and includes material that was omitted in the original release due to the limitations of an LP format. After listening to the Friday and Saturday night performances, it's hard to conceive of any musical effort that could top them, but it happened. Words prove inadequate to describe the music'stranscendence. It's a real credit to Jerry Wexler, Arif Mardin, and engineer Jean Paul (Les Paul's son and an outstanding recording engineer in his own right) that so much of the feeling of that night came through on the recording. There were overdubs, but they were true to the experience of that night. Purdie recalls that it was like the whole stage was lifted from its foundation and floating over the audience. The rhythm section played a syncopation that felt less staccato and more relaxed; the groove was so strong that it must have taken everyone to a higher state of consciousness.

One of the most soulful instrumentals that night was on a song you wouldn't expect it on. No one has ever played the "Ode to Billy Joe" as soulfully as King Curtis played it that night. Purdie was at the heart of it, with what for him was an understated performance, but the ghost notes were flying. It was funk drumming of the highest order, and everyone responded. Preston played extended chords on the organ, while Dupree played a perfect rhythm guitar riff. It was seamless: The Memphis Horns, Jemmott on bass, and Curtis himself, who played a soprano sax with electronic augmentation that gave his tone a pleading timbre. The whole performance showed that soul music could be just as powerful when played softly as loudly.

The instrumental segment of the show never lagged, and when Aretha came on stage, the audience was completely energized. She opened with "Respect" and stayed pretty close to the script of her previous performances. "Dr. Feelgood" continued to cast a spell over the audience, but there was no prayer meeting. Instead, she moved immediately into "Spirit in the Dark." When the band hit the double-time section of the piece, the whole place was rockin'. Aretha gave the song the full treatment, as though the show were about to close. The crowd shouted, "More! More! More!" It was in a frenzy. Then it happened. Caught up in the moment and disregarding all sorts of contractual entanglements, Ray Charles decided to sit in.

Ray Charles had been headquartered in L.A., and upon getting word that Aretha Franklin was killing at the Fillmore West, he flew in his private jet to San Francisco, met with Aretha and the band, and then returned to L.A. Aretha had never met Charles, and she was ecstatic that he would make the trip to see her. They met at the Fillmore West, while a press conference and reception were to be held on the concert floor several hours before the Sunday night performance. Even then, a line of fans had formed practically around the block, waiting for the doors to open for a performance that was four hours away. The press conference almost didn't happen, as Ray Charles had changed his mind about coming. But then Charles decided that he wanted to see Aretha Franklin after all, as they had never met. Aretha was so excited to meet Charles that it showed all over her face. Charles told her he couldn't stay for the concert and left to return to L.A. But on his way back, he ordered his pilot to turn the plane around and fly back to San Francisco. He caught the last hour of the Sunday night show off stage. Neither Aretha nor the band knew he was there, but when Aretha finished "Spirit in the Dark," she spotted Ray in the wings and insisted he sit in with her. A second, totally improvised concert was about to begin.

In the newer release, you can hear Charles asking Aretha under the din of the crowd, "How does that slow part go?" Aretha plays a few chords, and Ray says, "Oh, I see. I got it." And indeed, he did. Aretha shouts into the microphone, "I discovered Ray Charles!" Charles doesn't really know the lyrics, so Aretha prompts him. He scats and shouts in the spirit, so to speak. It's in the manner of talking in tongues but in rhythm. Aretha tells the band, "Stay right here! Stay right here!" The band continues to repeat a two-bar phrase in the pulsating groove, while Ray and Aretha banter back and forth. Finally, Purdie breaks the piece down with a fill of accented 16th notes, ending with a flam on the one. The band drops its volume and The Memphis Horns rest, but not for long. Now Curtis solos on his tenor, then Aretha on the electric piano. The volume is slowly building, and The Memphis Horns are back in the piece. Preston hits his gospel stride, as his fingers dance on the organ keys in the rhythm. Aretha offers the electric keyboard to Ray. "Will you do it for us, Ray?" Ray accepts. "You know I'll do anything for you, baby." Purdie breaks down the piece again, and the band again drops to a lower volume. Ray sits at the keyboard and starts rockin' back and forth. Charles had always had an exquisite feel in the tempos he sets, and he was hell on drummers who didn't get it right the first time. (In fact, before he died, Charles gave an interview to <u>Rolling Stone Magazine</u>. He was ill and in his last days. When asked if he had any regrets, he said that he wanted to apologize to the musicians he'd been so hard on, especially the drummers. Charles was driven by his musical vision and drove everyone around him to realize what only he could see, but the rhythm of his phrasing was clearly at the heart of it.)

Ray solos and asks his delirious audience over and over, "Can you feel the spirit?" He breaks the piece down one last time and then takes the piece home with the whole ensemble and the audience urging him on. The concert ends with "Reach Out and Touch (Somebody's Hand)," as Aretha proclaims, "What can you say about Ray Charles except he's sure enough the right reverend, ain't he?" Ray Charles was the artist who had brought thinly disguised church music into R&B fifteen years earlier with his breakthrough hit "I Got a Woman." The black church was horrified at the turn of events and tried to shut Charles down, but the horse was out of the corral, and there was no putting him back in.

It had been an exhilarating but exhausting night for Purdie and the whole band. What was to have been a two-and-half hour concert had stretched to almost four hours without a break. The energy level just kept getting higher and higher, and, of course, the adrenaline was flowing throughout the performance. One fan, organist and New York TV personality John Hammond, declared that the concert had changed his life. He had come to the concert a folk music accordion player but had left the Fillmore West dedicated to making a career in jazz and soul music. Hammond went on to fulfill his ambition on the B3 organ, the guitar, and the accordion.

There must have been many in the audience who recognized the concert as a once in a lifetime event. After Franklin's album was released, Purdie was asked to autograph the album cover by fans who had been there that night and who would bring their album with them wherever Purdie was playing a gig. Some even pointed out where they had been in the audience on the wide-angle photograph displayed on the inner cover. This enthusiasm continued for years after the concert was held.

Atlantic Records released two albums from the Fillmore West performances. <u>Aretha Live at Fillmore West</u> and <u>King Curtis Live at Fillmore West</u> were both hit albums and heralded the ascendancy of the long-playing album over the 45-rpm single as the dominant format of the recording industry. To this day, the Fillmore West concert remains the most exciting live performance Purdie ever played. Aretha Franklin has been cited as saying that this concert was a high point in her performing career. Jerry Wexler gives the event the same treatment in his biography. <u>Rolling Stone's</u> review of <u>King Curtis Live at Fillmore West</u> reads:

LET THE DRUMS SPEAK!

"...[Purdie] takes a drum break that literally explodes in your face. It lasts all of 20 seconds but is so positively electrifying it reduces me to uncontrolled laughter thinking about the hours that other drummers will put in trying to learn it. [Jerry] Jemmott and Purdie are very possibly the tightest, the most aggressive, the kickingest bass and drums combination in rock & roll today and for the rest of the album. Purdie succeeds in putting more different licks in the right place at the right time than all the drummers playing on all the albums in the Billboard Top Ten combined. [Jemmott] Keeps up with Purdie's bass drum as if the two men were tuned into the same great transistor control room in the sky, which is whispering (or shouting, as the case may be) the perfect signals for the perfect combinations into their ears. There are moments on the record where I wish they had taken everything else off and just left us these two geniuses working out." September 16, 1971

Purdie was on top of the world. For him it had been a dizzying ten-year climb, and now he sat at the pinnacle of the popular music world. He was at the top as a session drummer. He held the drum chair in the top band in the country, behind the top artist in the country. Purdie took a deep breath and smiled, satisfied with the decisions he had made and the course he had followed. He had weathered the flap with Jerry Wexler, and he and Curtis were thicker than thieves.

To Purdie, Curtis was Leonard Heywood and Cap rolled into one. Curtis was more than a bandleader: he was family, and that's how they got on. They would shoot pool, but with Purdie being more skillful at the game and Curtis too competitive to accept Purdie's dominance, Curtis would practice feverishly and then challenge Purdie to a rematch. Curtis did improve, but he still couldn't beat Purdie, who gloated over each victory, infuriating Curtis.

By August of 1971, both live albums had been released. Curtis began working on John Lennon's album Rock 'n' Roll. He cut a live album at the Montreux Jazz Festival and then went out on a short tour with Aretha that took his band through his home state of Texas. While in Texas, Purdie had trounced Curtis so soundly at pool that Curtis had a pool table installed in his new home on the upper west side of Manhattan just for a rematch. Purdie had invited Curtis and his family to a cookout at his place in the Pocono Mountains in mid-August. The night before the cookout, Curtis called Purdie for driving directions and the subject of pool came up again, with the usual good-natured trash talking between the two men.

Early the next morning Purdie drove into the city to pick up some items for the cookout, and as he was entering the Bronx on the expressway, he heard a series of King Curtis recordings on his car radio, being played one after the other. He was enjoying the music and thinking to himself how great it was for Curtis to get such airplay, when the disc jockey took a station break with, "We'll return with our tribute to the late King Curtis after this." A drug addict had stabbed Curtis to death on Friday the thirteenth on his own stoop, only minutes after Purdie had hung up the phone the night before.

As <u>Rolling Stone Magazine</u> reported it, Curtis's death at age thirty-seven was as absurd as it was sudden. Curtis was stabbed once in his chest and had pulled the knife from his own heart and stabbed his attacker four or five times. Curtis died. His attacker lived. Purdie doesn't remember how he drove his car to the shoulder of the highway, but it must have been an alarming maneuver. A number of motorists stopped their cars and approached his car to find Purdie muttering, "He's dead! He's dead!" The motorists asked him who was dead. Purdie couldn't answer. He just started crying.

17.

HEAVY IS THE HEAD THAT WEARS THE CROWN

King Curtis was more than a highly acclaimed bandleader; he was the man through whom many of the great R&B and rock talents of that era had come to Atlantic Records. He was practically a one-man A&R department, and there was an exceptionally long list of artists Curtis helped along the way. Curtis came to New York City from Fort Worth, Texas, in 1952, at the age of eighteen with his saxophone in a paper bag. A very talented reed player, Curtis had turned down several college scholarships to play with Lionel Hampton's band. Now he was playing sixteen record dates a week in New York and burning himself out for $40 a session. So, he raised his minimum rate to $100 a session and cut his schedule to eight sessions a week. He eventually recorded hits for other artists, includingthe Coasters' "Yakety Yak," in whic his honking tenor sax mimicked the voice of a nagging mother to her teenaged son. Some music critics believe that it was Curtis who really made the record a hit. Looking to record a hit of his own, Curtis teamed up with Bobby Robinson, a shoeshine man–turned–record producer, and the result was "Soul Twist," issued on Robinson's Enjoy label. Curtis's instrumental went to number one on the R&B charts.[30] He was a savvy businessman with an extraordinary network of relationships in and outside the record business.[31] Very down to earth, he was also a true prince of the city and was treated like royalty wherever he went. Purdie remembers that Curtis was one of the few people he knew who triple-park in Harlem on a Saturday night could, leave his keys in the car with the doors unlocked, and never have a problem. He had great influence in the music industry, and his untimely death was an occasion for mourning in many quarters.

On the day of his funeral, Atlantic closed its offices. It fell to Purdie to tend to many of the funeral arrangements. Of course, everyone who was anyone wanted to perform, to speak, or to have a special role at the funeral, and Purdie had the unenviable role of massaging the egos of artists who thought they should be included in the program. The Reverend Jesse Jackson presided, and the Kingpins played an hour-long rendition of "Soul Serenade," as mourners entered the sanctuary for the viewing. Services were held at St. Peter's Lutheran Church on Lexington Avenue, the internationally regarded "jazz church" of Manhattan.[32] There were thousands of people in the church and outside listening to the service on loudspeakers. Purdie was able to accommodate most of the instrumentalists wishing to pay their musical respects by arranging for them to sit in at various points in the one hour "Soul Serenade" musical prelude. Dizzy Gillespie, Ornette Coleman, Tyree Glenn, and Herbie Mann were among those who sat in. Political dignitaries, including the governor of New York State, the mayor of New York City, and various other state and federal officials, also attended.

Purdie cleverly placed all the singers in the choir box, where they sang with church choirs from Harlem and Newark, New Jersey. The Sweethearts of Soul and a vocal group called Tender Loving Care were also part of the choir. Donny Hathaway, Roberta Flack, Stevie Wonder, Brook Benton, Arthur Prysock, Chuck Jackson, Cissy Houston and her aunts Dionne and Dee Dee Warwick, and Joe Tex were in the choir. Stevie Wonder sang "Abraham, Martin, and John," and Aretha sang the closing spiritual "Never Grow Old," accompanied by Wonder on harmonica. The funeral procession followed a route through Curtis's beloved Harlem to a cemetery on Long Island, as was his wish. As a coda, Aretha Franklin paid tribute to Curtis in a full-page ad in Rolling Stone on the occasion of being named Singer of the Year 1971 by the National Association of Television and Radio Artists. It read:

"With a great deal of admiration, I will always remember my dear friend and conductor, KING CURTIS. His wonderful smile and friendship shall always be treasured among my most precious memories."

ARETHA

After the funeral, Franklin met with Atlantic executives to chart her musical course after the loss of King Curtis. They knew that Curtis was irreplaceable, but they wanted to hold the Kingpins together as a band. Curtis had often relied on Purdie to rehearse the band and with his obvious leadership abilities as a contract musician and bandleader in his own right, he was an obvious candidate from within the group. Whether Purdie could hold the band together after the loss of Curtis was another matter. Only time would tell. Purdie was offered the job, and he accepted it.

But Purdie would not have Curtis's deal with Atlantic. Curtis had a six-figure contract and the freedom to produce whatever he wanted to. Purdie would be paid as musical director of Franklin's road band by her management. The future of the Kingpins as a road band now depended heavily on Franklin's touring schedule. The Kingpins had never been just a road band to begin with. Curtis had kept them playing at Small's Paradise as often as his schedule permitted, thus keeping the players in New York much of the time, available to do session work for producers inside and outside of Atlantic. Being on the road was a grind. It might be energizing for the first week, but after that it could be a struggle. Playing the same material every night and living out of a suitcase was not exciting.

Moreover, on the road, Purdie was directing an eleven-piece band with a full horn section of three saxophones, a trombone, and two trumpets. Essentially, the rhythm section was Purdie, Cornell Dupree, Poncho Morales, Jerry Jemmott on bass, and Truman Thomas on piano, with Richard Tee subbing on occasion. The sax section was Ronnie Cuba, baritone; George Dorsey, alto; and Harold Vick, tenor. Kiane Zawadi on trombone and Danny Moore on trumpets made up the brass section. Chuck Rainey later replaced Jemmott, who had joined Roberta Flack's band.

No one could really fill the shoes of King Curtis. The Kingpins went on as a band, held together by the memory of King Curtis and the prestige of Aretha Franklin. But it wasn't long before the strain of Curtis's death manifested itself. As Curtis's shoes were too big to fill, all the band members took out their frustrations on Purdie, but the band stayed together, driven by Franklin's touring schedule and the excitement of the performances.

Whether Curtis's death influenced the timing of Franklin's next recording decision is unclear, but she decided to do something she had been urged to do for some time—record an album of gospel classics. In January of 1972 the New Temple Missionary Baptist Church in South Central Los Angeles was temporarily converted into a live recording studio. With gospel legend Reverend James

Cleveland at hand, leading the Southern California Community Choir, and a rhythm section including Bernard Purdie, Chuck Rainey, Cornell Dupree, and Poncho Morales, it was destined to be a historic endeavor. The audience was the full church congregation, which included gospel legends Clara Ward and her mother, Gertrude. John Hammond wrote in the album liner notes:

"It is wonderful to think that Aretha could be the very first singer to have a career both within and outside the church. Gospel congregations have rarely in the past forgiven singers who left them for the world of commerce. But from this album it is obvious that Aretha has been and will be welcome back with resounding hosannas."

The album went into the Billboard top ten, which was unheard of for a gospel recording. The last song was "You'll Never Grow Old," the song with which she had closed King Curtis's funeral service.

Through it all, Purdie still maintained a furious pace as a session musician. The year 1972 proved to be one of his most productive for new releases. That year he produced two albums under his own name, <u>Shaft</u> (Prestige) and <u>Soul Is . . . Pretty Purdie</u> (Flying Dutchman), and played on albums by B.B. King, Curtis Mayfield, Gabor Sabo, Grover Washington, Jr., Hank Crawford, James

Brown, Houston Person, Esther Phillips, Eddie "Cleanhead" Vincent, Donnie Hathaway and Roberta Flack, Oscar Brown, Les McCann, Leon Thomas, and Gil Scott-Heron. Purdie hired an office manager to keep his engagements on track. Purdie would fly back from the road to squeeze in various recording sessions when he had the opportunity. It was a very busy and lucrative time for him. But in 1973, something unexpected changed the picture.

On a flight to Detroit, Aretha Franklin's plane hit a severe air disturbance that threw her from her seat. The plane landed safely, but she vowed never to fly again—a vow she has kept to this day. This drastically altered her concert schedule and dramatically decreased the frequency of her performances. Franklin could afford it, but her musicians could not afford huge gaps between engagements.

Purdie remained her band director, but other members of the original Kingpins gradually left. Chuck Rainey went to Los Angeles. Cornell Dupree returned to Texas. Purdie started looking for opportunities to supplement his income and began an entrepreneurial aspect of his career that was littered with disappointment. He tried his hand at running a small record label owned by a respected record producer, only to have some rather thuggish-looking gentlemen arrive one day to shut the operation down. He took a shot at importing musical instruments from overseas, but he and his partner had irreconcilable differences that led to the breakup of the business. He was still recording, but the number of calls he got was on the wane. Still, in 1973 and 1975 he backed up Hall and Oates on their Atlantic debut album, <u>Abandoned Luncheonette,</u> played with the Three Degrees on their self-titled initial outing on Philadelphia International Records, and kept company with the likes of Quincy Jones, Gato Barbieri, Lou Donaldson, Richard "Groove" Holmes, and Joe Cocker. But the times, they were a' changin'.

In the 1970s Purdie accepted an unprecedented number of calls to overdub other artists' recordings. He became a ghost drummer on many recordings for which he would receive no public credit. These sessions paid more money, but one of the understandings in these arrangements was that he remain a ghost and not reveal his role in the production. Later, he would chomp at the bit because of this limitation, even disregarding it. In part this was due to his distaste for the manipulation of appearances to maintain false images of who did what for the public. As he saw it, the practice was too reminiscent of the days when the industry would cover the work of black artists with white faces. Of course, sweetening was a legitimate means of improving a recorded performance and was employed black on black, white on black, black on white, and white on white, too. Still, the creative anonymity rankled him, even though at times it was difficult to determine which tracks survived until the release of the recording. Such ambiguities grew exponentially as recording technology distorted the relationship between artistic performance and commercial product. More and more the artistic sensibilities of the record producer and the recording engineer were inserting themselves in the process until there was a musical shift in which recordings became the artistic elements employed in a wholly new art form, a form of aural collage that became known as hip-hop.

Purdie was no stranger to movie soundtracks. He had recorded the soundtrack for <u>Fritz the Cat</u> (MGM/UA, 1972), a ribald animated feature that followed the randy adventures of a lascivious feline, becoming the first animated film to earn an X-rating. He had also recorded the soundtrack to Galt MacDermot's <u>Cotton Comes to Harlem</u> (UA, 1970) a witty, urbane comedy about two black New York police detectives who track down a fast-talking, drug-dealing preacher who has smuggled drugs into the city in a bale of cotton. In 1974 Purdie was approached to write and perform in the soundtrack to <u>Laileh</u>, the first black X-rated movie ever produced. Now a collector's item, a copy of the vinyl album was listed for $1250 at The Sound Library record store in lower Manhattan in 2003.

As his session work began to slow in the mid 1970s, Purdie got the opportunity to tour with English rock star guitarist Jeff Beck. Beck's Blow by Blow Tour promoted his album of the same name. Beck was (and still is) a real rock star of the guitar god variety whose contemporaries were Jimmy Page and Eric Clapton. Coming out of legendary English groups like the Yardbirds, Beck had a huge international following of the "We can fill Wembly Stadium" variety. Keyboard player Max Middleton recommended Purdie for the tour, and Purdie in turn brought in bassist Wilbur Bascomb. Traditionally, the drummer's preference in bass players is honored. Middleton and Purdie had been playing together in the studio band Hummingbird on the A&M label. Hummingbird had disbanded, freeing Purdie and Middleton for the tour.

Purdie had never lived so well on the road as he did on the Blow by Blow Tour. The best hotels, a generous per diem, and everything first class was the rule; he and his bandmates traveled the world as superstars. Rod Stewart, Beck's singer before going solo, opened for Beck on tour. Purdie continued to do sessions whenever the tour schedule permitted. He saved his tour money to fund his next business project. He also continued to play with Aretha Franklin, but he was about to embark on a series of session projects that would imprint his artistic trademark on the mind of the music listener with a force equal to that of his association with her.

18.

STEELY WHO?

Although they have not had a number-one single or a number-one album, Steely Dan is a musical phenomenon. Compositions are filled with ambiguity, clever irony, and an irresistable blend of jazz, blues, and pop. Because their music is such a unique marriage of lyrics, melody, and harmony, other groups rarely covered their songs. Walter Becker and Donald Fagen make up Steely Dan. They are songwriters, lyricists, arrangers, performers, and masterful record producers. Their obsessive recording style is the most demanding in all musicdom, and they are particularly fussy about drummers. They seek the perfect fit between the stylings of individual session musicians and their material, and they don't stop recording until they get what they want. Session musicians are the creative material through which their musical visions are realized.

Fagen and Becker, kindred musical spirits from the New York suburbs, met at Bard College, a small liberal-arts school nestled among the mansions of the Hudson River Valley ninety miles north of Manhattan. Both men love jazz, the blues, and popular music, and both intensely dislike touring. So, after three commercially successful albums to their credit, they left their road band and proceeded to become studio hermits—all composing, producing, recording sessions, and releasing album, but no touring to promote the latest release. In the studio, a musical laboratory for this duo, Steely Dan polished their tracks beyond perfection and into a realm of high art.[33] It's what you might expect from two English majors from Bard College. Not only do their compositions comprise complex and literate ideas, but also as producers they take a thoughtful approach to session work.

"We realized we needed session musicians who had a larger palette of things they could do [and] who were also good readers, because they were coming in cold."[34] [35] – Donald Fagen
They never organized a stable studio band of their own like the Kingpins had been with Atlantic, or the Funk Brothers at Motown, or Booker T. and the MGs at Stax Records. Instead, they reached back to the approach of Duke Ellington. It is said that Ellington composed with individual musical personalities of his musicians in mind. Ellington wouldn't just write a part for the tenor saxophone; rather, he wrote a part for his specific tenor saxophonists—Johnny Hodges and Ben Webster—that would exploit their particular strengths. Becker and Fagen became acutely aware of the differences in session players' musical personalities, including regional differences. Comparing West Coast session players and those in New York, Becker observed that the West Coast musicians

were very savvy and precise in their approach to recording sessions, but

"... at the same time the New York session musicians had a musical style or sort of a hard-hitting attitude, or they took chances in their performances in a way that didn't happen on the West Coast."[36] — #Walter Becker

Although they didn't necessarily compose with a particular musician in mind, they sought out the musical stylings of individual session players whom they believed would give them the interpretation they wanted, and they seemed to know precisely what they wanted before the tracks were laid. But knowing your destination and knowing the route are not the same, so they would use their session time to audition soloists, rhythm sections, and horn sections in various combinations until they were satisfied.

"It wasn't like they played musical chairs with the guys in the band; they played musical bands. A whole band would go and a whole new incredible other band would come in."[37] — Rick Marotta, session drummer

And in the context of this reaching for ideal tracks:

"Most of the scrutiny was on the drummer. What they really wanted was to get great drum tracks."[38] — Dean Parks, session guitarist

So, in addition to being known for great compositions and great arrangements, Steely Dan became known in the drumming world as a crucible in which few were called and even fewer were chosen.

Steely Dan released seven albums to critical acclaim during its first eight years. During its three-year touring period, the band released Can't Buy a Thrill (1972), Countdown to Ecstacy (1973), and Pretzel Logic (1974), after which they released Katy Lied (1975), The Royal Scam (1976), Aja (1977), and Gaucho (1980). Then they stopped recording. Becker and Fagen went their separate ways to undertake individual projects. The separation lasted nineteen years. Fagen released two solo albums during this period, The Nightfly in 1983 and Kamakiriad in 1993. Steely Dan reunited in 2000 with its release of Two Against Nature in 2000 and Everything Must Go in 2003. In the intervening nineteen years, there was still a lot of interest in the reclusive Becker and Fagen. What made their music so compelling and fresh? One publication that took on the question was Modern Drummer Magazine. Founded in 1977 by drummer Ron Spagnardi, an alumnus of the prestigious Berklee School of Music in Boston, Modern Drummer was the first national magazine in the United States devoted exclusively to drums and drumming.

In a 1992 <u>Modern Drummer</u> article by Ken Micaleff, "The Drummers of Steely Dan," Bernard Purdie was front and center. Musically, Steely Dan was at the intersection of rock and roll, R&B, and jazz. Other groups had approached that same intersection from various directions. Jazz groups inspired by Miles Davis's conception called it fusion. Rock groups like Chicago and Blood, Sweat & Tears played pop/rock with horns and somewhat more considered arrangements in an attempt to add more interesting harmonies and other compositional devices to their music. But only Steely Dan had achieved a true amalgam.

"It was the most seamless joining of jazz and pop that there'd ever been. There's nothing else quite as sophisticated as that in all of rock music."[39] – Andy Gill, journalist

It really isn't rock music, just like it isn't really jazz or blues or rhythm and blues. Rock and pop are marketing categories, not musical ones. If the work is broadly popular, it's considered pop. If the music appeals to the rock audience, then it's rock music. And of course, rock and pop are where record companies want to be commercially because of the big dollars in those audiences. Fagen is unambiguous when he says, "I like black music whether it's jazz, R&B, or gospel." That is his inspiration. But he also likes television and film soundtrack music—"fake jazz," as he calls it. He and Becker bring a bohemian sensibility to black music, and they have the gifts to pull it off. Because they're white and popular, their music is classified as pop/rock; but their music is really a thing unto itself. The crucible of this new thing draws in session players from many parts of the musical spectrum, and Purdie is stacked up against the most accomplished drummers in the business. It's not a matter of who is better, but it does present an opportunity to judge Purdie's influence on popular music in its broadest sense.

The article gives Purdie his props. He's described as the Pharaoh of Funk, with grooves that "float and sting effortlessly above, below and through the music.... [It's] the stuff of legend."[40] Purdie was no stranger to <u>Modern Drummer Magazine</u>. He made the cover of the November 1985 issue, sharing it with Herb Lovelle, Grady Tate, and Ralph MacDonald.

The most emotional reaction in "The Drummers of Steely Dan" came from the late Jeff Porcaro, a drummer of immense talent and popularity who died tragically of a heart attack at the age of thirty-eight. His father, jazz drummer Joe Porcaro, tried to give a young Jeff lessons, but his son was so independent that he decided to just jump in the water and either sink or swim. He swam. When asked about his amazing technique, Jeff Porcaro said that he had none. "Anyone would sound good if they were playing twenty hours a day," and off he went, into a rant in his interview. It upset him that too many young drummers didn't know Bernard Purdie's musical contribution, when Purdie was the musical fountainhead of the drum sound they were most excited about.[41]

* * *

It's an early spring evening when we load Purdie's long, low 1996-Cadillac Fleetwood and leave his modest duplex in the New Jersey suburbs for Manhattan. Purdie's made the trip into Manhattan a million times. He knows just when to leave to avoid major traffic delays and at the same time have the best chance for on-street parking. The trip into the city is like a dream, as we crest the heights above the Hudson River to see the Manhattan skyline framed by a stunning sunset. We're headed for a chic nightclub called Le Bar Bat.

Le Bar Bat is in a converted stone church with stained-glass windows whose gothic architectural motif lends itself to the club's subterranean theme. The club's clientele are sophisticated young adults attracted by the prospect of a Steely Dan experience to be delivered by a tribute band and at least one member of the 1970s Steely Dan recording unit. Purdie's appearance is central to the promotion of the event, since neither Fagen nor Becker will be there that evening. Purdie enjoys headliner status, even though he continues to play the musical role of a sideman. But people will come out just to experience even a taste of the musical magic that inhabits the Steely Dan recordings of the 1970s, and Purdie is expected to deliver the magic that night without a rehearsal.

We drive up in front of the club's velvet rope and unload his equipment. Purdie is ushered into the club as the staff greets him with a mixture of reverence and awe. It is early, and the club is practically empty. The band had a sound check earlier that afternoon, but we appear to be the first ones there for the performance. We order dinner from the menu. While waiting for dinner, Purdie does a sound check on the drums with the sound engineer. Purdie doesn't fuss too much over the sound. When he gets close to a sound that he's satisfied with, he fine-tunes it with his incredible touch. Gradually, Le Bar Bat begins to fill, as band members and fans approach him at the dinner table. About an hour before showtime, Purdie disappears to prepare himself mentally for his set. Fifteen minutes before the set he returns, and we take a table in the balcony. The club is now abuzz with conversations punctuated by the tinkling of glasses and flatware. The air is filled with the fragrances of perfume and cologne. The first set starts, but Purdie is still in the balcony with me.

The first set goes well. The renditions of Steely Dan compositions are faithful to the original recordings and the audience is attentive and appreciative. At the break Purdie leaves the balcony and greets the musicians who have just left the bandstand. Some are members of the tribute band, while others are local contract musicians. They all seem to know Purdie. You can see from the looks in their eyes that they are genuinely in awe of him. When the second set begins, you understand why. From the first hit, the whole venue lights up. There's that magic. It's as if the whole band has levitated five feet above the stage. There are those musical nuances. The audience responds. There are the shuffles, the ghost notes, and the perfect fills. The level of excitement in the club builds. There is that touch and that incredible feel. Everyone in Le Bar Bat realizes that they are witnesses to an incredible gift. We're not just happy to be there; we're grateful.

19.

M. C. BUGSY

By the latter part of the 1970s, young people's tastes in music were changing radically. R&B and rock and roll were giving way to hip-hop music, with its heavy reliance on sampling, sparse harmonic content, almost complete absence of traditional musicianship, and its radically altered production values. If a rapper wanted Bernard Purdie on his record, he merely took a beat from one of Purdie's many recordings and sampled it. He didn't need Purdie, and he didn't need to pay Purdie. The effect was devastating to Purdie's recording career and to the studio system of record producers, arrangers, contract and session musicians, and engineers as a whole. Many of the recording studios closed as digital recording techniques and the new music allowed some artists to create entire recordings from the bits and pieces of past performances on vinyl or tape. These new recordings were aural collages that rearranged past performances in interesting patterns as backgrounds for the rhythmic poetry called rap. There was no room for Purdie's talent in this musical world on any consistent commercial basis.

Thus, his recording work began to slow. There were still live performances, work in the clubs, and the occasional recording session, but the halcyon days of wall-to-wall studio work were over. Still, the evidence of Purdie's musical influence was everywhere. The hi-hat chirps, his funky beats, his powerful rhythmic groove, and the memories they engendered were still in demand. When he looked back at his body of recording work, he knew that there were very few who could match his productivity. From the demos to the 45-rpm singles to the commercial jingles and the long-playing albums, Bernard Purdie was the most recorded drummer in the world. He was still working with Aretha Franklin and getting calls for individual musical projects. He had several musical groups with which he worked regularly: The Three Bs, with pianist Bross Townsend and bassist Bob Cunningham; The Hudson River Rats, with vocalist and harmonica virtuoso, Rob Paparozzi; The Masters of Groove, with organist Reuben Wilson and guitarist Grant Green, Jr.; and Purdie's Powerhouse, out of Portland, Oregon. Also, Galt MacDermot's New Pulse Band was still performing and recording. (In fact, the band performs at Carnegie Hall every December.)

The power of hip-hop lies in its chemistry of percussive rhythm and poetry. Its roots may be in an ancient African art form mastered by court performers called <u>griots,</u> who were both musicians and keepers of tribal history, lore, and genealogies, which they were trained to recite flawlessly while performing traditional forms of musical accompaniment. Of course, popular songs have lyrics that tell stories, but the stories themselves derive their power from the melody, with the exception of country songs and folk songs, whose lyrics often transcend their melodies. A griot is more troubadour than pop singer. His material comes from the experiences and history of his people. There is an epic reach in the recitations, and the poetry of the recitations is more story than lyric. Speech has a rhythm of its own, and the musical style of folk music is profoundly influenced by the style of the spoken word. The placement of accents and the pronunciation of words and phrases influence the stylistic tendencies of musical composition. By contrast, in hip-hop, the musical accompaniment is typically sparse, and the poetry is encased in a rigid meter that follows a familiar pattern of bars and choruses that makes the music accessible to a popular audience while the verbal acrobatics in the telling of the story playfully dance around the repetitive musical theme. In its rhythmic form, hip-hop is as rigid as the Japanese haiku, while the meter of its poetry can be as challenging as the most complicated be-bop phrasing.

As with any "new thing," hip-hop has its antecedents, its roots. In the late 1960s those roots showed in the emergence of artists who had something urgent and angry to express. The assassination of President Kennedy in 1963 in Dallas, the Vietnam War draft, the assassination of Martin Luther King, Jr., in Memphis in April 1968, and the ensuing race riots followed by the June 1968 assassination of Democratic presidential candidate Robert Kennedy started a fire in a group of black poets from Harlem who dubbed themselves the Last Poets. Consecrating their artistic collaboration on the birthdate of Malcolm X in East Harlem's Marcus Garvey Park, the Last Poets went on a verbal rampage in a scathing polemic against white supremacy ("The White Man's Got a God Complex") and black complacency and dysfunction ("Niggers Are Afraid of Revolution," "Black People What Y'all Gon' Do?"). Douglas Records released The Last Poets in 1970, followed by This Is Madness in 1971.

Shortly after The Last Poets released, another poet/vocalist released his first album, Small Talk on 125th and Lennox Avenue (1971) on the Flying Dutchman label. The poet, Gil-Scott Heron, based his first album on his volume of poetry of the same title. Heron's style is polished, and his material is filled with satire and wit. Heron played the piano and sang as well. His material often blurs the lines between poetry and song. He was very popular, with several tracks reaching the upper levels of the popular charts, which was quite an accomplishment for an Afrocentric artist.

In 1971 the poet Nikki Giovanni released Truth Is on Its Way. Now a professor of English and black studies at Virginia Tech, Giovanni delivered her poems to the stylings of the New York Community Gospel Choir. In one very popular track, "Ego Tripping," she is accompanied by nothing more than a bass drum, a tambourine, hand claps, and some vocal encouragement ("Right on, sista!," "Yeah!"). On the bass drum was Bernard Purdie, who played it like Yo-Yo Ma plays the cello. Drumming is about many things, but with Purdie, it's surely about touch, which he displays magnificently on that track. (Look, Ma: no hands).

Purdie recorded with all three of these artists in the early 1970s.[42] It seems that when a more contemporary and less tribal African drum sound was needed, Purdie got the call. The irony is that rap would move away from its Afrocentric roots as it became more commercial, and, ultimately, it embodied the very black caricatures lampooned by its early founders. The unabashed money, lust, and abuse of women touted in the new rap were a complete surrender to the very stereotypes that earlier rap artists were straining to escape. Heron later recorded a rebuke of the content of hip-hop and rap lyrics as they emerged in the 1980s and 1990s. The editor-in-chief of Wax Poetics, a quarterly journal on hip-hop culture, also lamented the turn that hip-hop had taken away from political relevance.

BERNARD PURDIE

"Now you can't go anywhere on this planet and not hear hip-hop, because it's universal. This is something from kids born in the ghettos of the Bronx. Nobody gave a damn about these kids, and they turned that negative energy into something positive. It's created a multibillion-dollar industry all over the world. If hip-hop had some sort of direction . . . I think it's the record companies' goal to keep it dumb, to keep it stupid, because that's what sells records. The closest we ever got to some sort of direction in hip-hop was Public Enemy back in like the late '80s and early '90s, where you could see the people coming together. But I think that you don't hear much about them now because they became a threat. There is potential for hip-hop to become a really big political movement and to unite kids from all over the world. You have Japanese kids getting their hair cornrowed. This is more than just liking a song. They identify with our struggle." — Andre Torres

Purdie's licks survived the change through the sampling of his many rhythm tracks. Although sampling was of limited commercial value to Purdie, it proved the universality of his distinctive sound; he crossed over to be embraced by a new generation of musicians who utilized his sound in an entirely different musical context. <u>Wax Poetics</u> wrote a cover article on Purdie in its second issue. As its editor, Andre Torres explained that hip-hop disc jockeys were always on the lookout for funky break beats, which they would mine from vinyl albums. Many of these albums were obscure recordings, but once the word got around that an album with Purdie on it was likely to yield a rich vein of sampling material, DJs stampeded to prospect for these rhythmic nuggets. Purdie had become a hip-hop superstar, albeit a secret one whom only insiders knew about.

20.

THE RINGO STARR CONTROVERSY

In 1963 advance work was under way to introduce an obscure English band into the United States market. The band's manager arranged to update the sound of some of the band's early recordings with musical arrangements customized to American musical tastes. Purdie was called in to overdub the drummer on twenty-one tracks of these recordings. The songs were nice, but the name of the group meant nothing to him at the time. Purdie was paid both for his contribution to the effort and to keep his mouth shut. The group was the Beatles, who in January 1964 appeared on <u>The Ed Sullivan Show</u> and turned the world of popular music upside down. The country fell insanely in love with the four mop tops from Liverpool, England. The seismic cultural impact moved some social critics to observe that the arrival of the Beatles on American shores signaled the end of the country's period of mourning over the assassination of young, charismatic President John F. Kennedy, who had been shot in his Dallas, Texas, motorcade just months earlier.

Purdie kept his mouth shut for fifteen years until, while teaching a music course at The New School, some of his students began holding up Ringo Starr as one of the greatest drummers of his era.

Although Purdie didn't remember which specific tracks he had overdubbed, he couldn't let such a statement go unchallenged. Purdie told his class that it was he who had played on the early Beatles recordings. As soon as the words left his mouth, Purdie knew that he had stepped on a hornet's nest. There followed a series of magazine and radio interviews that gave Purdie's claim wider circulation. By this time the Beatles' spectacular trajectory of fame and fortune had run its course, and they had been proclaimed by many as the most popular music group in the second half of the twentieth century, if not of all time. Not only was their domination of the record charts unprecedented (in 1964 they held the top five spots simultaneously), but the compositions of Lennon and McCartney were already classics being recorded and performed many times over across the musical spectrum, from symphony orchestras and jazz bands to lounge acts. The Beatles broke up in 1970, six short years after they first appeared in the United States, but their legion of fans are as unswerving in their devotion, as any fans, perhaps with the exception of Elvis Presley fans.

Without question, the hornets, whose nest Purdie had stepped on, were furious. During a radio interview, one caller made a death threat, and years later, when e-mail was widely available, threats were sent to Purdie's website. The Internet has extended the life of the controversy, with e-mail threads extending into late 2004. Some are humorous, such as the comment, "Purdie is a jive turkey. Love his drumming." Others take an academic approach, meticulously picking at Purdie's claim. Then there are the facetious e-mails charging Purdie with claiming to be the ghost performer for every drummer from Buddy Rich to Dennis Chambers. As of October 2004, a Google search under "Beatles Purdie" yielded 1,410 threads. Purdie never claimed he had sweetened any but the earliest Beatles recordings. Whether the overdubbed drummer was Pete Best or Ringo Starr is also open to question. Purdie didn't know the individual musicians on the recordings at the time. It's unlikely that the controversy will be resolved to the satisfaction of Ringo Starr fans or Purdie fans. Starr doesn't comment on the matter. Is it a tempest in a teapot? After all, everyone is subject to sweetening, even Purdie. Purdie is the first to admit it. It's a part of show business. Anonymity is the price that session players pay for the privilege of the great variety of work they often enjoy and the challenge of shaping musical raw material. Purdie would not have been happy playing in a single group. Perhaps there is some vindication of Purdie's role with the Beatles. In 1978 the feature-length film <u>Sgt. Pepper's Lonely Hearts Club Band</u> was released. It was a tribute to the music of the Beatles, starring the Bee Gees and Peter Frampton, with Bernard Purdie on drums.

PART IV

THE PURDIE EFFECT

21.

WHAT IS FUNK?

As Purdie's stature began to grow among studio players and record producers, the inevitable questions arose about how Purdie's playing was unique. After all, if Purdie's playing could be reduced to a formula, he could be musically cloned. Purdie was not a reluctant teacher of his style, but at his level of musicianship, each player has a signature sound, and like fingerprints no two are exactly the same. Each performance emanates from a singular musical personality. Purdie's musical personality, as that of any musician, was shaped by his innate sensibilities, his musical influences, his technique, and a thousand other mysteries.

Also, there is no accounting for the unique qualities of a particular talent. Rhythm is all around us, but rhythm is also within us. For example, the tempo of our breathing and the pattern of our speech are individual to each of us. Purdie's style of playing is reflected in the way he walks and dances and moves about. Of course, Purdie's playing quickly became an influence on up-and-coming drummers drawn to his style. Like spice in a stew, his influence began to flavor the performances of other musicians, not just other drummers. Composers and arrangers began to imagine the Purdie "flavor" in their own musical recipes. So, what began as the inspiration of an individual musician spawned an entire genre of music.

It is not clear who invented funk. It is not clear what funk is. But it is clear that the name of Bernard Purdie is never very far from the word "funk" in the conversations of musicians and music lovers. It is also clear that another name may be closer than Purdie's in the public mind: James Brown. Brown coined the term and created the paradigm, but Purdie brought the people the good news.

As much as artists may protest the categorization of art, category[43] can be an honest reflection of what the public experiences when exposed to an innovative style. Music is a language beyond words, yet the intellect cannot resist the temptation to rationalize it. Why is there a mystery about music that defies our rational understanding? After all, music has substance. The string vibrates. The air vibrates. The inner ear vibrates, sending electrical impulses to the brain. Music is physical. Music is physics. So, what is the mystery? After that stream of electrical impulses enters the brain, then what?[44] Perhaps music connects with the world on a spiritual level that can be experienced but not reduced to concepts. If we mortals manage to capture the essence of music in the spoken word, will the magic of it vanish and all rejoicing in it cease? Probably not. Leonard Bernstein observed that poetry is word music. To the Greeks poetry was a musical form, not a literary one. What then of lyrics or opera? Does this word "music" merely share in the elements of instrumental music, or does it open up the possibility of rationalizing its mysteries? Such questions have baffled philosophers for centuries. Is it possible to construct some narrative model that might describe funk with an acceptable degree of accuracy? That is doubtful, but its musical form can be described.

Funk music is a form of rhythm and blues that is closely identified with soul music. Soul music is rhythm and blues as it evolved in the 1960s and 1970s—the predominant style of black popular music until hip-hop and rap created an abrupt shift in the evolution of black music in the early 1980s. It is performed at a moderate tempo in 4/4 time (although Purdie showed in his Purdie Shuffle how it could be played with a half-time shuffle feel using partial triplets woven into a steady backbeat). Purdie's style is not confined to funk drumming, but the groove element is prevalent in all his playing and informs his funk rhythms as well. When asked by a young Japanese fan how he did a groove, Purdie described it as an undercurrent that has a positive feel. "A groove comes out of a positive attitude. You don't have to be loud. You can be subtle. But you have to know where the 'ONE' is." Funk music has a distinct quality because of its subtle dynamics, which improved recording techniques were able to capture.[45] In funk, the traditional backbeat is eclipsed as the focal point of the dynamics by a regular emphasis on the first beat of every measure or every other measure. There is also a prominent feeling of locomotion in the rhythm (CHUGA, chuga, Chuga, chuga, CHUGA, chuga, Chuga, chuga) that encourages a movement of rocking back and forth rather than side to side.

There is no doubt that Purdie spread the funk sound to every corner of the recording world. If funk is a disease, Purdie is Typhoid Mary. In everything Purdie plays, there is a measure of funkiness, even if the material is not funk per se. And where there is a measure of funkiness, there will always be a party.

22.

PURDIE WISDOM

<u>On Teaching the "Purdie Feeling"</u>

"What I've been told is that I play to join everybody, to pull everybody in and just pick them up and carry them whichever way it has to go. That's the gift that I have. I realize that that is my gift, so I'm not telling people that everybody is going to do that, but don't tell me that you can't teach feeling. This is the thing that I had been fighting for forty years, almost fifty years. People say, 'Well, you can't teach feeling.' I say that's wrong. Of course, you can. Of course, you can, but the feeling that you're going to teach has got to come from that individual. You show the student how to make it, and then you're going to end up getting his feeling or her feeling, not mine. Ninety-eight percent of all the students that come to me have bad habits because they've been watching others over the course of the years. See, years ago there weren't videos, so you had to listen very, very carefully to what was being played, and then you had to try to re-create on your own what you thought you heard and what you're creating. But in today's world you don't have to. Go buy a video and see what they're doing. And then you feel like you got it. But you don't because all you're doing now is mimicking who that person is. You haven't tapped yourself. That's what I have. That's what I do. I'm not going to try to play Steve Gadd or Billy Cobham or anybody. I play what I play because I'm an individual. I'm an individual, but I happen to be one with 'that thing,' as they call it."

On Ego

"I have the gift to give my thing back to people immediately, not next week, next month, next year, but NOW! They've been telling me this all my life, and personally I thought they were just telling me that to shut me up 'cause I was asking too many questions. I needed to know. I was always asking something. And I really thought that that's what it was for me, but I learned so much and I realize that I do have the gift. But how can you be modest about something that you know that you have? And the answer for me was, all right, it's a job. I have a job to do, you go do your job. You got the gift, do your job, you're getting paid for it, do your job, and that way it throws my ego out the window.

We all have egos, and we need them. We need them just to play because we need to satisfy not only ourselves, but we need to satisfy our inner selves to get it out to people and let people know what we have to offer. So, I need them to know that I got something to say, I want you to listen. I am not going to try to say what Steve Gadd has said or what he is doing; I'm not going to try to play Louie Bellson; I'm not going to try to play Billy Cobham. They all have their own individual things that they say. I have something to say, so my inner self needs to come out, so I work at doing just that and that's how I get along with everybody. In other words, you got to learn to be humble, because people do not want to be around a know-it-all, but somebody who says it and does it. I had to learn that the hard way from so many different people. I have ticked off a lot of people in this business because I did what I said that I was going to do. I wasn't saying it as a matter of ego; it's just something that I can do. To me it was still a job, but always be the best that you can be at it. I'm good at what I do, but I'm still going to be even better because what I try to do is pull everybody with me as I'm doing it. When that happens, all the rest of the people go with me. And you can't miss me. I'm going to be right in everybody's face, and that means you can't lose me when it comes down to mixing and editing in the music. I'm going to pull everybody, so we are so tight there's no way that you're going to lose me. That's what I have learned. That's what I know that I have. I have that particular kind of gift that anybody that sits down and plays with me— I'm going to love them to death. We all need our egos stroked and to do whatever has to be done so that we can move on to the next step. But if we can control our egos, we can do anything, especially in music."

On Still Dreaming (After All These Years)

"I stopped being bitter over twenty years ago. I stopped being bitter about people f—ing over me. All right, I didn't have everything there that I should have, didn't retain what I needed to retain. Ah, you trusted people. Can't blame anybody but yourself. So, I got good at what I'm doing, so I started doing a little less and watching a little bit more, and as I did that I saw where some of the mistakes that I made were, so I wouldn't go right back in the same pitfalls—same hole. That was hard. That was hard lessons 'cause it was costly. Believe me. You find it, and you bear it. Now—and please don't get me wrong in what I'm about to say—I believe that people are sincere when they make an offer about wanting to do something. Their intentions are good, are honorable. Something happens, it just happens, and it falls by the wayside. Nobody's fault, but the point is that I had to learn to listen to what you had to say, say thank you and move on, and then if it does happen all good and fine, then I can say thank you two or three times because the point is that I'm not going to sit here and wait for you to go do something, but meanwhile I'm going to continue and try to fulfill my own dreams and do it."

On "The Concept"

"[Music is marketed in categories.] There was Latin funk and folk rock. Then there was jazz funk (long before jazz fusion, jazz). But I was just crossing all the borders. The point is that all of them wanted dance music. They wanted the beat. All of these groups wanted the beat because they wanted folks to dance. But that's what I call all of my music—dance music. I've always called it that. I never called it jazz music, rock music, rhythm and blues music, funk music. To me it was just a job. Mr. Heywood taught me very early in my life never limit myself to one kind of playing. You go with the flow of the music. I didn't know I was playing rock, jazz, blues, funk, soul, country, hillbilly, New Orleans, march music. It was just music to me. I know it's hard to explain, but to me it was strictly, strictly music. I have never put a category on music, except music. I like all kinds of music, so why can't I play it. That's what I've always said because I can see it[46]. It's all about a concept. That's how I was taught. Everything is a concept. The notes are not going to change. The only thing that changes is the rhythm, and if you understand the rhythms of the music, you can play it. A quarter note is a quarter note. An eighth note is an eighth note. A sixteenth is always going to be a sixteenth note. But how you interpret it is where the rhythms come in. It's all a concept. That's why when I forced the Purdie Shuffle on people, it took years for them to understand that all I was doing was motivating people and moving people. The people could feel it, but they didn't know what it was. And nobody else was doing it, so they kept coming back to me. That's why so many demos that I made became hit records. They tried to re-create records and they couldn't do it."

23.

THE PURDIE LEGACY

Bernard Purdie is now seventy-two years old, and he remains a very active musician. He records, plays club dates, teaches, and conducts clinics all over the world. He's very popular in Japan, Germany, Great Britain, Brazil, Italy, Spain, and Africa, where his reputation as a legendary drummer remains strong. On occasion, he gets calls from younger artists who want that live Purdie sound on their recordings, but for the most part, the commercial focus of the record industry has passed on to a new generation. Atlantic Records was sold decades ago, spinning off new labels and promoting a new generation of music artists. Yet Purdie still leads a very exciting musical life, because his ability to groove never fails to excite audiences. The Purdie magic is still there.

Bernard Purdie's playing has touched millions of people over the last half-century. In the first third of his career, after arriving in New York, Purdie was a secret superstar, recording in public obscurity on R&B tracks that, when released as singles or even as cuts on albums, did not identify him or the other session players. The producers, artists, engineers, and session players knew what Purdie was doing, but the general listening public did not. His was the peculiar anonymity of a virtuoso instrumentalist who hired himself out for recording purposes and then moved on to a new session, a different artist, a different record company, a new producer. He was one of the many musical nomads not associated with any particular musical organization. As a result, a large body of his work is not associated with him in the public mind, even though it has been immensely influential. It is fair to say that of the R&B artists with significant hits from 1964 to 1974, there are very few who did not have Purdie on one or more of their recorded tracks. Purdie built his studio reputation not on the hit records the public associated him with, but on the ones that the public has no idea that he contributed to. This was long before publication of the first issue of <u>Modern Drummer Magazine</u>. Only studio insiders knew of Bernard "Pretty" Purdie as the hit-maker, unless they happened to read the 1968 <u>New Yorker</u> article.

When Atlantic Records released Aretha Franklin's <u>Young, Gifted and Black</u> in 1971, with the track "Rock Steady," the general public took notice of Purdie. A few months later her <u>Aretha Live at Fillmore</u> sealed Purdie's reputation. The Steely Dan recordings introduced him to rock fans who were blown away by Purdie's musical energy and originality. But drummers and other musical artists are very aggressive about tracking down players who have a sound and a feel that attracts them. There was a buzz about Purdie among the cognoscenti, and the influence of his sound began to spread. Drum teachers were listening as their students began to express interest in Purdie's sound. Serious young players began to seek him out for instruction. The next generation of musical superstars was laboring in obscurity, laying the foundations for their own unique sounds; when those sounds matured and emerged, there was often an immense Bernard Purdie cornerstone to their own performances. These drummers— Jeff Porcaro, Dennis Chambers, David Garibaldi, Kenny Aronoff, Steve Gadd, John Bonham, and Steve Smith—would themselves become legends. The Purdie feel would emerge in artists as disparate as Devo and Billie Joel. Jazz drummer T. S. Monk, son of Thelonious Monk, called Purdie "the Art Blakey of Rhythm and Blues." Legendary drummer Mickey Roker called Purdie the "Elvin Jones of R & B." When the great singer Michael McDonald was asked what drummer, he regretted not having worked with, he named Bernard Purdie. In the wake of Purdie's constant artistic striving, he shaped the course of the music he loved so much.

24.

HOME AT LAST

In the spring of 2006, Union County, New Jersey, celebrated Purdie's sixty-fifth birthday with a birthday bash in Cedar Brook Park called Rhythm and Blues by the Brook. The musicians who come to pay tribute to Purdie's fifty years in the music business turn a summer park concert into a happening.

In the lobby of once-segregated Elkton High School, a plaque reads:

> Bernard Purdie
> Class of 1960

In the world of stars and superstars, Bernard Purdie is the wizard they all look to—to mix and meld the rhythms needed to translate into gold and platinum recordings and solid radio and video hits. It is the drum tracks he created for Prestige records on countless LPs with a multiplicity of organists, saxophonists and guitarists that has made Bernard Purdie into somewhat of a prophet among record collectors in Japan & Europe.

He is well aware that the business side of popular music calls for accomplished technicians who can "deliver the goods"—or in his case, subdivide the beats to improve the rhythm"—whether scoring films, playing in Broadway musicals, recording performing folk, funk, fusion, Latin, psychedelic rock, gospel, soul, pop-rock, classical high art music R&B, country, carnival and circus music.

He has over 4,000 albums to his credit, along with extensive road experience with great musicians and entertainers. Among those he has toured and recorded with are: Dizzy Gillespie, Steely Dan, King Curtis, James Brown, Aretha Franklin, the Beatles, Paul Simon, Roberta Flack, the Monkees, Herb Alpert, Count Basie, Duke Ellington, the Rolling Stones, Hall & Oates, Paul Simon, B.B. King, Brook Benton, Percy Sledge, Branford Marsalis, Harry Connick, Jr., John Williams and the Boston Pops (with Nell Carter as soloist, and an 80-piece gospel ensemble).

Aretha's hit song "Rock Steady" from the album Young, Gifted & Black (Atlantic) blew everybody's minds in 1972. But as far as drum history is concerned, the song contained the much-replicated Bernard Purdie signature hi-hat lick. The same album contains the song, "Day Dreaming," which is a totally different side of Bernard's playing and just as brilliant. It features little snare side-stickings and is Bernard's version of a reggae groove. Also on the same album is a song called "Brand New Me," which reveals his fabulous shuffle. No Purdie hit list would be complete without some Steely Dan albums. <u>The Royal Scam</u> (ABC) from 1976 brilliantly captured his groove abilities.

Purdie returns and speaks to a music class in the band room. Then he asks for volunteers for a musical experiment in improvisation. Purdie plays, and each volunteer plays piano, with remarkable results.

In the summer of 2004, the extended Purdie family had a family reunion in Elkton. James, Cap, and Mary lie in unmarked graves in a disheveled cemetery just off the grounds of the now-defunct George Washington Carver public school for the colored children of Cecil County. The reunion was held in a building off Route 40, where young Bugsy used to work the marriage trade. Just across the road is the Elkton Diner, still in operation, where James and most of the Purdie children worked at one time or another. Everybody brought a dish, and there are children, grandchildren, and even a few great grandchildren. Purdie played with a group of local musicians who are completely in awe of him. At age sixty-two, the Purdie musical fire burned as brightly as ever, perhaps even a little brighter on that particular afternoon. On the riser behind the drums with his head thrown back, his eyes closed and an ecstatic expression on his face, Bugsy was a joy to behold. Bernard Purdie was home at last.

THE END

(L-R) James Henry Purdie Jr., Grandfather Captain Jack (Wesley Jackson) and Father James Henry Purdie

Bernard "Bugsy" Purdie Graduation Picture
Elkton Senior High School Class of 1960

Grandma McNeill

(Top L-R) Yvonne Queen,
Mary Emma McNeil
(Bottom L-R) Aunt Ruth, Grandma

Bugsy 1959

Bugsy 1960
High School Graduation

(L-R) Tommie, Ernie, Bernard (Bugsy) Grandma, Henry, Richard (Hedgie), Nate, and Aunt Ruth

Nate, Hedgie, Bernard, James III, Henry, Ernie, and Tommie Purdie

(L-R) Nate, Thelma, Henry, Ernie, Tommie and Betty Purdie

(L-R) Thelma, Dolores and Betty Purdie

(L-R) Yvonne Queen, Aunt Ruth, Bernard, Dolores and Mary Emma McNeil

Nate and Ernie Purdie

Clyde Bessicks and Dolores Purdie

"Pretty" Purdie and B.B. King
(Photo Courtesy of Drummer World)

"The Thrill Is Gone"
(Photo Courtesy of Dino Perrucci)

(L-R) Cornell Dupree, Chuck Rainey, Aretha Franklin
and Bernard Purdie (Photo courtesy of Chuck Rainey)

(L-R) Tommie, Ernie, Bernard (Bugsy) Grandma, Henry, Richard (Hedgie), Nate, and Aunt Ruth

Nate, Hedgie, Bernard, James III, Henry, Ernie, and Tommie Purdie

Galt MacDermot and Bernard Purdie - "Hair"

Bernard Purdie onstage - "Hair"

Rythym Section - "Hair"
(L-R) Galt MacDermot, Bernard Purdie,
David Spinozza and Wilbur Bascomb

"If your ego is big enough and you show self-confidence, someone is going to give you a shot."

Band Picture - "Hair"

Galt MacDermot's New Pulse Jazz Band

Steely Dan - Donald Fagan, Bernard Purdie, Walter Becker, Paul Griffin and Chuck Rainey

From the DVD "The Making of Aja"

Rob Paparozzi and Bernard Purdie

Bernard and Rob - Hudson River Rats

Hudson River Rats - (L-R) Rob Paparozzi, Bernard Purdie, George Naha and John Korba

Bernard and Rob
Hudson River Rats

Hudson River Rats
with Chuck Rainey and Tim Timko

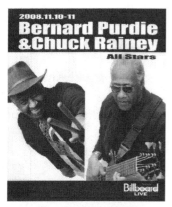
Purdie-Rainey Coalition
in Japan

(L-R) Rob Paparozzi, Chuck Rainey,
Bernard Purdie, George Naha
and Jeff Young in Japan

Winston Byrd, Bobby Boyd, Will Calhoun,
Purdie and Jason "Malletman" Taylor

Godfather's of Groove
Ruben Wilson, Grant Green Jr.
and The Pretty One
(Photo Courtesy of Rick Gilbert)

David Haney and Purdie

(L-R) Cornell Dupree, Jerry Jemmott,
Herbie Lovelle and Purdie

Will Lee and Purdie

Purdie and T.M. Stevens

Purdie and Taj Mahal

Guitar Virtuoso Frankie Cicala and Purdie
(Photo courtesy of The Asbury Park Press)

Singer, songwriter and guitarist
Jack Hoban with Purdie

Pianist Miho Nobuzane, Purdie and
Bassist Tetsuya Sato

Soul Catcher - Leslie Gray, Tim Hearn,
Purdie, Shea Marshall and Mahlon Hawk

Purdie, Rob Paparaozzi,
Frank Pagano and Melvin Sparks

50 years of "L
The Drums S

APPENDIX

DISCOGRAPHY

A PARTIAL LIST OF JAZZ ARTISTS BERNARD "PRETTY" PURDIE HAS ACCOMPANIED[47]

TOP 100 R&B ARTISTS[48] BERNARD PRETTY PURDIE HAS ACCOMPANIED

COUNTRY & WESTERN HALL OF FAME ARTISTS BERNARD PURDIE HAS ACCOMPANIED.

A PARTIAL LIST OF POPULAR ARTISTS BERNARD PURDIE HAS ACCOMPANIED.

A Partial List of Jazz Artists Bernard "Pretty" Purdie Has Accompanied[49]

John Abercrombie; Port Chester, NY
Brian Abrahams; Capetown, SA
George Adams; Covington, GA
Pepper Adams; Highland Park, IL
Cannonball Adderly; Tampa, FL
Nat Adderly; Tampa, FL
Bernard Addison; Annapolis, MD
Toshiko Akiyoshi; Darien, Manchuria
Monty Alexander; Kingston, Jamaica
Geri Allen; Pontiac, Michigan
Henry "Red" Allen; New Orleans, LA
Pete Allen; Newbury, Bershire, UK
Mose Allison; Tippo, MS
Gene Ammons; Chicago, IL
David Amram; Philadelphia, PA
Cat Anderson; Greenville, SC
Ernestine Anderson; Houston, TX
Louis Armstrong; New Orleans, LA
Art Ensemble of Chicago
Dorothy Ashby; Detroit, MI
Harold Ashby; Kansas City, MO
Roy Ayers; Los Angeles, CA
Albert Ayler; Cleveland, OH
Benny Bailey; Cleveland, OH
Buster Bailey; Memphis, TN
Pearl Bailey; Newport News, VA

Chet Baker; Yale, OK
Ginger Baker; London
Gato Barbieri; Rosario, Argentina
Eddie Barefield; Scandia, Iowa
Charlie Barnet; New York City, NY
Ray Barreto; New York City, NY
Kenny Barron; Philadelphia, PA
Gary Bartz; Baltimore, MD
Count Basie; Red Bank, NJ
Alvin Baptiste; New Orleans, LA
Sidney Bechet; New Orleans, LA
Louie Belson; Rock Falls, IL
Tony Bennett; New York City, NY
George Benson; Pittsburgh, PA
Bob Berg; Brooklyn, NY
Tim Berne; Syracuse, NY
Walter Bishop, Jr.; New York City, NY
Eubie Blake; Baltimore, MD
Art Blakey; Pittsburgh, PA
Terrence Blanchard; New Orleans, LA
Carla Bley; Oakland, CA
Jane Ira Bloom; Newton, MA
Arthur Blythe; Los Angeles, CA
Claude Bolling; Cannes, France
Earl Bostic; Tulsa, OK
Michael Brecker; Philadelphia, PA

Randy Brecker; Philadelphia, PA
Dee Dee Bridgewater; Memphis, TN
Bob Brookmeyer; Kansas City, MO
Ray Brown; Pittsburgh, PA
Vernon Brown; Venice, IL
Tom Brown; Queens, NY
Dave Brubeck; Concord, CA
Bill Bruford; Sevenoaks, Kent, UK
Ray Bryant; Philadelphia, PA
Ralph Burns; Newton, MA
Kenny Burrell; Detroit, MI
Gary Burton; Anderson, IN
Joe Bushkin; New York City, NY
Billy Butterfield; Middleton, OH
Jaki Byard; Worcester, MA
Don Byas; Muskogee, OK
Charlie Byrd; Suffolk, VA
Donald Byrd; Detroit, MI
Nick Caiazza; New Castle, PA
Red Callender; Haynesville, VA
Cab Calloway; Rochester, NY
Candido Camero; Havana, Cuba
Harry Carney; Boston, MA
Benny Carter; New York City, NY
Betty Carter; Flint, MI
Ron Carter; Femdale, MI
Al Casey; Louisville KY
Geoff Castle; London, UK
Lee Castle; New York City, NY

Joe Chambers; Stoneacre, VA
Paul Chambers; Pittsburgh, PA
Ray Charles; Albany, GA
Doc Cheatham; Nashville, TN
Stanely Clarke; Philadelphia, PA
Buck Clayton; Parsons, KS
Jimmy Cleveland; Wartrace, TN
Rosemary Clooney; Maysville, KY
Billy Cobham; Zurch, Switzerland
Alan Cohen; London, UK
Al Cohn; Brooklyn, NY
Richie Cole; Trenton, NJ
George Coleman; Memphis, TN
Ornette Coleman; Fort Worth, TX
Johnny Coles; Trenton, NJ
Buddy Collette; Los Angeles, CA
Graham Collier; Tynemouth, UK
Alice Coltrane; Detroit, MI
Ravi Coltrane; Huntington. NY
Eddie Condon; Goodland, IN
Harry Connick, Jr.; New Orleans, LA
Ray Conniff; Attleboro, MA
Junior Cook; Pensacola, FL
Chick Corea; Chelsea, MA
Larry Coryell; Galveston, TX
Stanley Cowell; Toledo, OH
Ray Crane; Skegness, UK
Bob Cranshaw; Evanston, IL
Hank Crawford; Memphis, TN

Ray Crawford; Pittsburgh, PA
Gary Crosby; London, UK
Stanley Crouch; Los Angeles, CA
Ted Curson; Philadelphia, PA
King Curtis; Fort Worth, TX
Dave Dallwitz; Adelaide, Australia
Franco D'Andrea; Merano, Italy
Eddie Daniels; New York City, NY
Maxine Daniels; London, UK
Eddie "Lockjaw" Davis; NYC, NY
Miles Davis; Alton, IL
Nathan Davis; Kansas City, KS
Richard Davis; Chicago, IL
Walter Davis, Jr.; Richmond, VA
Wild Bill Davis; Glasgow, MO
Alan Dawson; Marietta, PA
John D'Earth; Holliston, MA
Buddy DeFranco; Camden, NJ
Jack DeJohnette; Chicago, IL
Paul Desmond; San Francisco, CA
Vic Dickenson; Xenia, OH
Al Di Meola; Bergenfield, NJ
Dirty Dozen Brass Band, NO, LA
Bill Doggett; Philadelphia, PA
Lou Donaldson; Badin, NC
Kenny Drew; New York City, NY
Ray Drummond; Brookline, MA
George Duke; San Rafael, CA
Ted Dunbar; Port Arthur, TX

George Duvivier; New York City, NY
Teddy Edwards; Jackson, MS
Mark Egan; Brockton, MA
Roy Eldridge; Pittsburgh, PA
Duke Ellington; Washington, DC
Mercer Ellington; Washington, DC
Don Ellis; Los Angeles, CA
Herb Ellis; McKinley, TX
Rolf Ericson; Stockholm, Sweden
Peter Erskine; Somers Point, NJ
Kevin Eubanks; Philadelphia, PA
Gil Evans; Toronto, Canada
John Faddis; Oakland, CA
Georgie Fame; Leigh, UK
Art Farmer; Council Bluffs, AK
Joe Farrell; Chicago, IL
Victor Feldman; London, UK
Maynard Ferguson; Montreal, Canada
Ella Fitzgerald; Newport News, VA
Tommy Flanagan; Detroit, MI
Jimmy Forrest; St. Louis, MO
Sonny Fortune; Philadelphia, PA
Frank Foster; Cincinnati, OH
Pete Fountain; New Orleans, LA
Charlie Fowlkes; New York City, NY
Panama Francis; Miami, FL
Aretha Franklin; Memphis, TN
Jack Free; London, UK
Bill Frisell; Baltimore, MD

Curtis Fuller; Detroit, MI
Steve Gadd; Rochester, NY
Eric Gale; New York City, NY
Jim Galloway; Kilwinning, UK
Hal Galper; Alem, MA
Erroll Garner; Pittsburgh, PA
Kenny Garrett; Detroit, MI
Jimmy Garrison; Miami, FL
Leonard Gaskins; Brooklyn, NY
Herb Geller; Los Angeles, CA
Terry Gibbs; Brooklyn, NY
Dizzy Gillespie; Cherw, SC
Tyree Glenn; Corsicana, TX
Benny Golson; Philadelphia, PA
Eddie Gomez; Santurce, PR
Babs Gonzales; Newark, NJ
Jerry Gonzales; New York City, NY
Dexter Gordon; Los Angeles, CA
Danny Gottlieb; New York City, NY
Benny Green; New York City, NY
Freddie Green; Charleston, SC
Grant Green; St. Louis, MO
Urbie Green; Mobile, AL
Sonny Greer; Long Branch, NJ
Al Grey; Aldie, VA
Johnny Griffin; Chicago, IL
Henry Grimes; Philadelphia, PA
Tiny Grimes; Newport News, VA
Bobby Hackett; Providence, RI

Charlie Haden; Shenandoah, IA
Jim Hall; Buffalo, NY
Chico Hamilton; Los Angeles, CA
Jimmy Hamilton; Dillon, SC
Scott Hamilton; Providence, RI
Lionel Hamilton; Louisville, KY
Slide Hampton; Jeanette, PA
Herbie Hancock; Chicago, IL
Jake Hanna; Roxbury, MA
Sir Roland Hanna; Detroit, MI
Bill Hardman; Cleveland, OH
Roy Hargrove; Dallas, TX
The Harper Brothers, Brooklyn, NY
Tom Harrell; Urbana, IL
Barry Harris; Detroit, MI
Benny Harris; New York City, NY
Bill Harris; Philadelphia, PA
Eddie Harris; Chicago, IL
Hampyon Hawes; Los Angeles, CA
Coleman Hawkins; St. Joseph, MO
Erskin Hawkins; Birmingham, AL
Roy Haynes; Roxbury, MA
J.C. Heard; Daytona. OH
Albert "Tootie' Heath; Phila, PA
Jimmy Heath; Philadelphia, PA
Percy Heath; Philadelphia, PA
Joe Henderson; Lima, OH
Jon Hendricks; Newark, OH
Eddie Heywood, Atlanta, GA

John Hicks; Atlanta, GA
Billy Higgins; Los Angeles
Earl "Fatha" Hines; Pittsburgh, PA
Milt Hinton; Vicksburgh, Miss.
Al Hirt; New Orleans
Johnny Hodges; Cambridge, MA
Major Holley; Detroit, MI
Red Holloway; Helena, AK
Richard "Groove" Holmes; NJ
Paul Horn; New York City, NY
Shirley Horn; Washington, DC
Lena Horne; Brooklyn, NY
Freddie Hubbard; Indianapolis, IN
Eddie Hubble; Santa Barbara, CA
Daniel Humair; Geneva, Switzerland
Helen Humes; Louisville, KY
Alberta Hunter; Memphis, TN
Gary Husband; Leeds, UK
Bobby Hutcherson; Los Angeles, CA
Dick Hyman; New York City, NY
Dennis Irwin; Birmingham, AL
Chubby Jackson; New York City, NY
Milt Jackson; Detroit, MI
Illinois Jacquet; Broussard, LA
Bob James; Marshal, MI
Harry James; Albany, GA
Keith Jarrett; Allentown, PA
Clifford Jarvis; Boston, MA
Jazz Crusaders, Los Angeles, CA

Eddie Jefferson; Pittsburgh, PA
Paul Jeffrey; New York City, NY
Billy Jenkins; Bromley, Kent, UK
Papa Bue Jensen; Copenhagen, Denmark
Jerry Jerome; Brooklyn, NY
Budd Johnson; Dallas, TX
Gus Johnson; Tyler, TX
Howard Johnson; Montgomery, AL
J.J. Johnson; Indianapolis, IN
Marc Johnson; Omaha, NE
Sy Johnson; New Haven, CT
Etta Jones; Aiken, SC
Hank Jones; Vicksburg, MS
Jimmy Jones; Memphis, TN
Jonah Jones; Louisville; KY
Quincy Jones; Chicago, IL
Rodney Jones; New Haven, CT
Thad Jones; Pontiac, MI
Clifford Jordon; Chicago, IL
Ronny Jordan; London, UK
Stanley Jordan; Chicago, IL
Taft Jordan; Florence, SC
Roger Kellaway; Waban, MA
George Kelly; Miami, FL
Wynton Kelly; Kingston, Jamaica
Barney Kessel; Muskogee, OK
Steve Kahn; Los Angeles, CA
Kenny Kirkland; Brooklyn, NY

Earl Klugh; Detroit, MI
Lee Konitz; Chicago, IL
Gene Krupa; Chicago, IL
Billy Kyle; Philadelphia, PA
Cleo Lane; Southall, UK
Rick Laird; Dublin, Ireland
Oliver Lake; Marianna, AK
Lambert Hendricks & Ross, IL
Harold Land; Houston, TX
Yusef Lateef; Chattanooga, TN
Hubert Laws; Houston, TX
Ronnie Laws; Houston, TX
Brian Leake; London, UK
Peggy Lee; Jamestown, OH
Michel Legrand; Paris, France
Stan Levey; Philadelphia, PA
Rod Levitt; Portland, OR
John Lewis; La Grange, IL
Mel Lewis; Buffalo, NY
Ramsey Lewis; Chicago, IL
Willie Lewis; Cleburne, TX
Dave Liebman; Brooklyn, NY
Terry Lightfoot; Middlesex, UK
Kirk Lightsey; Detroit, MI
Abbey Lincoln; Chicago, IL
Melba Liston; Kansas City, MO
Alan Littlejohn; London, UK
Charles Lloyd; Memphis, TN
Joe Lovano; Cleveland, OH

Jimmy Lytell; New York City, NY
Johnny Lytle; Springfield, OH
Harold Mabern; Memphis, TN
Teo Macero; Glens Falls, NY
Machito; Tampa, FL
Dave MacRae; Auckland, New Zealand
Mike Mainieri; Bronx, NY
Junior Mance; Chicago, IL
Chuck Mangione; Rochester, NY
Manhattan Transfer, NYC, NY
Herbie Mann; Brooklyn, NY
Tania Maria; Sao Luiz, Brazil
Branford Marsalis; Breaux Bridge, LA
Wynton Marsalis; New Orleans, LA
Pat Martino; Philadelphia, PA
Hugh Masekela; Witbank, South Africa
Bennie Maupin; Detroit, MI
Jimmy Maxwell; Stockton, CA
Lyle Mays; Wausakee, WS
Cecil McBee; Tulsa, OK
Christian McBride; Philadelphia, PA
Les McCann; Lexington, KY
Ron McClure; New Haven, CN
Bob McCracken; Dallas, TX
Brother Jack McDuff, Champaign, IL
Bobby McFerrin; New York City, NY
Howard McGee; Tulsa, OK
Jimmy McGriff; Philadelphia, PA
Ken McIntyre; Boston, MA

Dave McKenna; Woonsocket, RI
Al McKibbon; Chicago, IL
Ray McKiley; Fort Worth, TX
Bill McKinney; Cynthiana; KY
Hal McKusick; Medford, MA
John McLaughlin; Kirk Sandall, UK
Jackie McLean; New York City, NY
John McLevy; Dundee, UK
Charles McPherson; Joplin, MO
Carmen McRae; New York City, NY
Jay McShann; Muskogee, OK
Johnny Mercer; Savannah, GA
Louis Metcalf; St. Louis, MO
Pat Metheny; Lee's Summit, MO
Butch Miles; Ironton, OH
Mulgrew Miller; Greenwood, MS
Johnny Mince; Chicago, IL
Charles Mingus; Nogales, AZ
Bob Mintzer; New Rochelle, NY
Blue Mitchell; Miami, FL
George Mitchell; Louisville, KY
Red Mitchell; New York City, NY
Hank Mobley; Eastman, GA
Wes Montgomery; Indianapolis, IN
Tete Montolu; Barcelona, Spain
James Moody; Savannah, GA
Airto Moreira; Itaiopolis, Brazil
Joe Morello; Springfield, MA
Frank Morgan; Minneapolis, MN

Paul Motian; Providence, RI
Alphonse Mouzon; Charleston, SC
Don Mote; Rochester, NYC, NY
George Mraz; Pisek, Czechoslovakia
Gerry Mulligan; New York City, NY
Jimmy Mundy; Cincinnati, OH
Ray Nance; Chicago, IL
Marty Napoleon; Brooklyn, NY
Phil Napoleon; Boston, MA
National Youth Jazz Orchestra
Joe Newman; New Orleans, LA
Red Nichols; Ogden, UT
Red Norvo; Beardstown, IL
Adam Nussbaum; New York City, NY
Helen O'Connell; Lima, OH
Anita O'Day; Chicago, IL
Chico O'Farrill; Havana, Cuba
Sy Oliver; Battle Creek, MI
Jimmy Owens; New York City, NY
Marty Paich; Oakland, CA
Eddie Palmieri; New York City, NY
Jackie Paris; Nutley, NJ
Maceo Parker; Kinston, NC
Joe Pass; New Brunswick, NJ
Jaco Pastorius; Norristown, PA
Les Paul; Waukesha, WI
Cecil Payne; Brooklyn, NY
Sonny Payne; NY
Duke Pearson; Atlanta, GA

Art Pepper; Gardena, CA
Bill Perkins; San Francisco, CA
Charli Persip; Morristown, NJ
Ralph Peterson; Pleasantville, NJ
Michel Petrucciani; Montpelier, France
Nat Pierce; Somerville, MA
Dave Pike; Detroit, MI
Courtney Pine; London, UK
Bucky Pizzarelli; Paterson, NJ
John Pizzarelli; Paterson, NJ
Lonnie Plaxico; Chicago, IL
Jean-Luc Ponty; Avranches, France
Andre Previn; Berlin, Germany
Sammy Price; Honey Grove, TX
Julian Priester; Chicago, IL
Brian Priestley; Manchester, UK
Bernie Privin; Brooklyn, NY
Russell Procope; New York City, NY
Tito Puente; New York City, NY
Don Pullen; Roanoke, VA
Flora Purim; Rio de Janiero, Brazil

Alton Purnell; New Orleans, LA
Ram Ramirez; San Juan, Puerto Rico
Bill Rank; Lafayette, IN
Joshua Redman; Berkeley, CA
Dizzy Reece; Kingston, Jamaica
Diane Reeves; Detroit, MI
Rufus Reid; Atlanta, GA
Buddy Rich; Brooklyn, NY
Lee Ritenour; Los Angeles, CA
Sam Rivers; El Reno, OK
Max Roach; New Land, NC
Jim Robinson; Deer Range, LA
Claudio Roditi; Rio de Janeiro, Brazil
Red Rodney; Philadelphia, PA
Sonny Rollins; New York City, NY
Bobby Rosengarden; Elgin, IL
Frank Rosolino; Detroit, MI
Charlie Rouse; Washington, DC
Ernie Royal; Los Angeles, CA
Marshall Royal; Oklahoma City, OK

Top 100 R&B Artists Bernard "Pretty" Purdie Has Accompanied

James Brown-1
Aretha Franklin-2
The Temptations-3
Stevie Wonder-4
[Louis Jordan-5]¹
Ray Charles-6
Marvin Gaye-7
Gladys Knight & The Pips-8
The Isley Brothers-9
Fats Domino-10
B.B. King-11
The O'Jays-12
Michael Jackson-13
Prince-14
Bobby Bland-15
Nat "King Cole-16
Dinah Washungton-17
Kool & The Gang-18
Four Tops-19
Earth, Wind & Fire-20
The Miracles-21
Dianna Ross-22
Luther Vandross-23
Janet Jackson-24
Whitney Houston-25
Jerry Butler-26
Barry White-27
The Impressions-28
Wilson Pickett-29
The Supremes-30
Jackson 5/Jacksons-31
Joe Simon-32
Dionne Warwick-33
Brook Benton-34
Jackie Wilson-35
The Whispers-36
Spinners-37

---

¹ Artists not accompanied by Purdie in brackets

Patti LaBelle-38
The Drifters-39
[Elvis Presley-40]
Smokey Robinson-41
Johnny Taylor-42
Tyrone Davis-43
Sam Cooke-44
The Dells-45
Parliament/Funkadelic-46
The Manhattans-47
Peabo Bryson-48
[Cameo-49]
Freddie Jackson-50
Bobby Womack-51
Al Green-52
Teddy Pendergrass-53
The Moments-54
[R.Kelly-55]
The Chi-Lites-56
The Gap Band-57
Commodores-58
Natalie Cole-59
Mariah Carey-60
[Keith Sweatt-61]

Stephanie Mills-62
Ruth Brown-63
Joe Tex-64
New Edition-65
Rick James-66
[Mary J. Blige-67]
The Dramatics-68
Ashford & Simpson-69
Donna Summer-70
Gene Chandler-71
[Bar-Kays-72]
[LL Cool J-73]
Chaka Khan-74
[Boyz II Men-75]
Otis Redding-76
Roberta Flack-77
Melba Moore-78
The Clovers-79
Betty Wright-80
Maze, featuring Frankie Beverly-81
[Rufus, feat. Chaka Khan-82]
Atlantic Starr-83
Millie Jackson-84

Chuck Berry-85

Tavares-86

Pointer Sisters-87

Curtis Mayfield-88

Levert-89

[Ohio Players-90]

George Benson-91

Lionel Richie-92

Ivory Joe Hunter-93

Lloyd Price-94

The Stylistics-95

Little Richard-96

Jr. Walker & The All Stars-97

Denece Wlliams-98

Hank Ballard & the Midnighters-99

Etta James-100

Top 100 R&B Artists Bernard "Pretty" Purdie Has Accompanied[50]

Barbara Acklin	Chairmen of the Board
Arthur Alexander	Ndugu Chancler
Ashford & Simpson	Gene Chandler
Patti Austin	The Chi-Lites
LaVerne Baker	The Chiffons
Florence Ballard	Linda Clifford
Fontella Bass	Arthur Conley
Brook Benton	Norman Connors
The Blackbyrds	Lou Courtney
Peggi Blu	Don Covay
Dee Dee Bridgewater	Caroline Crawford
Johnny Bristol	Hank Crawford
Brothers Johnson	Randy Crawford
James Brown	Steve Cropper
Jocelyn Brown	King Curtis
Oscar Brown, Jr.	Tyrone Davis
Keni Burke	Sam Dees
Solomon Burke	The Delfonics
Jerry Butler	The Dells
James Carr	Lamont Dozier
Jean Carne	The Dramatics
Diahann Carroll	George Duke

Dennis Edwards
Shirley Ellis
The Escorts
Fatback Band
Eddie Floyd
Inez & Charlie Foxx
The Four Tops
Aretha Franklin
Carolyn Franklyn
Erma Franklin
Friends of Distinction
Marvin Gaye
Al Green
Billy Griffin
Johnny Hammond
Donny Hathaway
Isaac Hayes
Holland-Dozier-Holland
Bobby Hebb
Jack Hoban
Jimmy Holiday
Loleatta Holloway
Eddie Holman
Cissy Houston

Thelma Houston
Phyllis Hyman
The Isley Brothers
The Jackson Five
Michael Jackson
Bob James
Grace Jones
Linda Jones
Tamiko Jones
Thelma Jones
Ronny Jordan
Margie Joseph
Chaka Kahn
Kid Creole & The Coconuts
Albert King
B.B. King
Ben E. King
Gladys Knight
Jeane Knight
Kokomo
Labelle Betty Lavette
Ronnie Laws
Linda Lewis
Ramsey Lewis

Lonnie Liston Smith	Esther Phillips
Little Anthony & The Imperials	Wilson Pickett
Little Milton	Courtney Pine
Jon Lucien	Billy Preston
Cheryl Lynn	Lou Rawls
The Manhattans	Martha Reeves & The Vandellas
Barbara Mason	D.J. Rogers
Curtis Mayfield	The Royalettes
Eugene McDaniels	Ruby & The Romantics
Van McCoy	The Sandpebbles
Wllie Mitchehell	Freddie Scott
Garnet Mimms	Gloria Scott
The Moments	Jimmy Scott
The Moments	Gil Scott-Heron
The Montclairs	Marlena Shaw
Sam Moore	The Shirelles
Mother's Finest	Nina Simone
Byron Motley	Percy Sledge
The O'Jays	The Spinners
Ray Parker, Jr.	Dusty Springfield
Billy Paul	The Staple Singers
Freda PaynePeaches and Herb	Mavis Staples
Ann Peebles	Edwinn Starr
Teddy Pendergrass	The Stylistics

Donna Summer

Syreeta

Tavares

Little Johnny Taylor

The Temptations

Joe Tex

Carla Thomas

Rufus Thomas

The Three Degrees

Ike & Tina Turner

Phil Upchurch

The Van Dykes

The Velvelettes

Dee Dee Warwick

Grover Washington, Jr.

The Whispers

Jackie WilsonNancy Wilson

Bobby Womack

Betty Wright

Norma Jean Wright

END NOTES

[1] Duke Ellington described the musical inspiration of his drummer, Sonny Greer, with this colorful phrase. Of Greer, Ellington wrote, "Instead of following in his father's footsteps, Greer apparently wasted his time banging on his mother's pots and pans, and he developed his own style of drumming from those bim-banging beginnings. A natural supporting artist with his pots and pans, he kept time with horses trotting, people sweeping, and people digging ditches. He didn't indulge in any of these activities himself, but he kept time with those who did."
<u>Music Is My Mistress</u>, Doubleday & Company (1973), p. 51.

[2] An example of this is the musical composition "Country Preacher" by Joe Zawinul, performed on the 1969 album of the the same name by the Cannonball Adderly Quintet.

[3] Words and music by Jimmy Driftwood.

[4] <http://ubl.artistdirect.com/music/artist/bio/0,400178,00.html?artist=Mickey+Baker>

[5] Nietzsche, F., <u>The Birth of Tragedy out of the Spirit of Music</u>, trans. Francis Golffing (Garden City, NY: Doubleday, Anchor Books, 1956.)

[6] Galt MacDermot, piano; Bernard Purdie, drums; Wilbur "Bad" Bascomb, bass; Allen "Wing" Wong, saxophone; Bill Easely, saxophone; Patience Higgins, baritone saxophone; Vincent MacDermot, trombone; John Frosk, trumpet; the late Seldon Powell, saxophone.

[7] Al Kooper, musician/writer/producer: "I was weaned at 1650 Broadway in NYC from 1958 to 1965. I started in the offices of Leo Rogers, an underhanded personal manager

with a great deal of charisma. 1650 was the 'real' Brill Building. 1619 Broadway was the 'actual' Brill Building, but 200 times more action and success took place in 1650. The 'actual' Brill Building was the last bastion of Tin Pan Alley and was widely regarded as an old man's building. Other than Leiber, Stoller, Bacharach, Barry, and Greenwich, everything else took place at 1650 Broadway. The problem was 1650 was just 1650; it had no title to hang any memorabilia on. So, the Brill Building gets all the credit, but that's completely false. In the offices of 1650: Paul Simon, Tony Orlando, Carole King, Gerry Goffin, Barry Mann, Cynthia Weil, Neil Sedaka, Lenny Bruce, Dionne Warwick, the Shirelles, Chuck Jackson, Aldon Music, Roosevelt Music, Allegro Recording Studios, Artie Ripp, Bobby Lewis, the Jive Five, the Cadillacs, the Isley Brothers, Aaron Schroeder, Gene Pitney, Luther Dixon, the Strangeloves, Bob Gaudio, End Records, Gone Records, Bell Records, Amy-Mala Records, Scepter Records, BelTone Records, Dimension Records, and yours truly. The education I received in that building for seven years far outweighs any university matriculation. The adjoining coffee shop, B/G, had the greatest pancakes in the United States. I commuted from Queens. Also from my neighborhood were the Temptations (the white version, with Artie Ripp) and Paul Simon and Artie Garfunkel. Nearby neighbors were bassist Harvey Brooks and pianist Paul Harris."
<http://www.randomhouse.co.uk/catalog/extract.htm?command=search&db=main.txt&eqisbndata=0099443651>
[8] Sammy Lowe had his heart set on playing professional baseball, but music became his favorite pastime and his ticket to the music major league. One of Birmingham's most prolific arrangers, Sammy was the chief arranger and composer for the Erskine Hawkins Orchestra for nearly twenty-two years. His list of monster hits with the band include, "Bearmash Blues," "Nona," "No Soap," "Midnight

Stroll," "Bicycle Bounce," and "Raid the Joint." His arrangement of "I've Got a Right to Cry" for Birmingham vocalist Laura Washington soared on the national charts in 1946. Sammy's big band swing days included gigs with bandleaders Cab Calloway, Lucky Millinder, Sammy Davis, Jr., Sy Oliver, and Don Redman. His rock 'n' roll days were spent arranging for The Platters, Al Hirt, Sam Cooke, The Isley Brothers, The Tokens, the Godfather of Soul, James Brown, and many others. Hirt called Sammy the "best arranger in the business." Sammy arranged Brown's 1966 million-seller record single, "It's a Man's, Man's, Man's World." His other million single recordings include The Tokens' "The Lion Sleeps Tonight," Sylvia's "Pillow Talk," Roy Hamilton's "You Can Have Her," and the Moments' "Sexy Mama."

Sammy Lowe was one of the charter members of the Alabama Jazz Hall of Fame in 1978, http://www.jazzhall.com/inductees/SammyLowe.asp.

[9] Tempo is essentially arithmetic (i.e., 1, 2, 3, 4 or 1, 2, 3, etc.), expressed in beats per minute. The pulse of the music arises in the performance and goes beyond tempo. It cannot be expressed in beats per minute. In percussion it is sometimes spoken of as playing "behind the beat" (jazz, blues, R&B), "on the beat" (rock 'n' roll, pop), or "on top of the beat" (Latin). These expressions are closer to the point. Purdie's expression that all music must breathe may be the best description of this phenomenon. Taking a hint from Leonard Bernstein, one could say that the pulse of a performance is the flow of its energy as it interacts with the tempo and harmonic and rhythmic structure of a piece. The complexity or perhaps the subjectivity of this musical calculus expresses a quality in music that is more organic than mathematical. It emanates from the musical personalities of the performers and their musical interaction

under the emotional spell cast by the composition as it unfolds.

[10] Quote from the Aja DVD.
[11] Danny Sims: Johnny Nash was a pop singer. But the firsjust one show, right? R&B record that I ever got him to do was called "Move and Groove". That record became #1 in the R&B market. A guy named Magnificent Donahue, a DJ from New York moved to LA, and we did a commercial with the track and we put it on every station in the country. And do you know what they put on the commercial? They put 'burn baby burn' and this record was #1 in Chicago and Watts and so the FBI called me and said 'Danny we finally got you, you are out of your mind, they are burning down Watts, they are burning down the cities.' We got on a plane and went to Jamaica, we moved to Jamaica. I didn't even know Bob Marley then, we had a distributor at Federal Records. Danny Sims: We went down there because we thought we were going to get killed by the CIA and the FBI. For 'inciting a riot' they called it. Detroit went down, Chicago went down, L.A. went down, the country just went up in flames and we were right in the midst of that. Jamaica was a place to get away from the shooting. <http://www.jahworks.org/dannysims.htm>

[12] Donald Fagan of Steely Dan recalls, "There's the famous story about Bernard in the early sixties. He'd come to the session and he'd have these two signs with him. He'd set up one sign on one side of the drum that would say, "You've Done It!," and the other sign on the other side of the drum would say, "You've Hired the Hit-Maker, Pretty Purdie!" It's that confidence that you need to get a good R&B track. The Greatest Records in Rock History: Steely Dan – "Aja" (Eagle Rock Entertainment, 1999 dvd).

[13] African Rhythm..., p. 34. {Is African Rhythm the name of a book?}

[14] The word *mambo* comes from the Ñañigo dialect spoken in Cuba. It probably has no real meaning, but occurs in the phrase *"abrecuto y guiri mambo"* ("open your eyes and listen") used to open Cuban song contests. In the Bantu language of West Africa, mambo means "conversation with the gods" and in nearby Haiti, a Mambo is a Mambo Mexicano.

In 1947, Prado left Cuba for reasons that are not completely clear. In his unpublished biography of Prado, Michael Mcdonald-Ross quotes Rosendo Ruiz-Quevedo as saying that Prado's incorporation of North American jazz into the mambo was fiercely resisted by certain elements of the Cuban musical establishment. Especially enraged was **Fernando Castro** , the local agent of the Southern Music Publishing Company and Peer International which had a monopoly of Cuban music publishing at the time. Mcdonald-Ross wrote, "Castro denounced Prado by stating that he was adulterating Cuban music with jazz. As a result, Prado's arranging assignments ended and, unable to continue to work in Cuba, he left, eventually to settle in Mexico." When Prado left Cuba in 1947, he embarked on tours which took him first to Buenos Aires, Argentina, then to Mexico, Panama, Puerto Rico, and Venezuela. Mcdonald-Ross called these tours "unrewarding," but other accounts say that he won the adulation of teenage dance fans, causing traffic jams and near riots wherever he played. voodoo priestess.
<http://www.laventure.net/tourist/prez_bio.htm>

[15] Ron Carter, bass; the late Tony Williams, drums; Wayne Shorter, sax. Davis's first quintet comprised Red Garland, piano; John Coltrane, sax; "Philly" Joe Jones, drums; and Paul Chambers, bass. This unit performed in 1955–1956.

[16] Santamaría was also a gifted composer. His composition "Afro Blue," made popular by Cal Tjader, is practically a jazz anthem.
[17] Columbia was organized soon after Thomas Alva Edison, the Wizard of Menlo Park, invented or at least perfected the phonograph in 1878. But, whereas Edison had seen the phonograph as a business machine used for dictation, the founders of Columbia had the vision to put their capital into producing recordings of music to be played on the device. Columbia grew to become one of the largest record companies of the twentieth century. Columbia changed its name to CBS Records and is now owned by Sony Music Entertainment.
[18] Wynton Marsalis. Ken Burns <u>Jazz: Episode I</u> (Florentine Films 2000 DVD)
[19] Steely Dan comment about confidence.
[20] Roy McCurdy-expand.{Are you going to expand?}
[21] A 1966 live recording, *King Curtis Live at Small's Paradise* has been re-released as part two album/two disc set on the Collectables label. The performances were recorded with Ray Lucas on drums, Chuck Rainey on electric bass, Paul Griffin on piano and Cornell Dupree on guitar. The other disc is a 1959 album of King Curtis with Belton Evans on Drums titled *HaveTenor Sax, Will Blow*.
[22] The Beatles concert at Shea Stadium is purportedly the first stadium concert ever held and set a trend that became commonplace for musical groups able to attract such huge audiences.
[23] {The typesetter will reinsert the image here. There is not enough memory to show it here.}

"WE WANT SLOOPY!"—Block O

"In 1965, an almost-unknown rock band from Ohio called

The McCoys recorded a song called "Hang On Sloopy." "Hang On Sloopy" was inspired by a woman named Dorothy Sloop, a native of Steubenville, Ohio. Apparently, she had a career as a singer in the 1950s and used the name "Sloopy" as a stage name. Dorothy Sloop passed away in Pass Christian, Mississippi. Her song will long live on in the hearts of Buckeye fans everywhere!

I'm sure the OSU Band had absolutely no idea of what it was about to start, but "Sloopy" soon became a lasting tradition in the Horseshoe on crisp Saturday afternoons in the fall in Columbus, Ohio. A band member named John Tatgenhorst first arranged "Hang On Sloopy" for the OSU Band. The band director, Dr. Charles Spohn, didn't really want to use it at the games, but finally Tatgenhorst persuaded him to let them play the song. So, on Saturday, October 9, 1965 during a rainy, muddy Ohio State/Illinois game, "Hang On Sloopy" made its football debut in the "Shoe." The first week, the song didn't really catch on, but during the second game the fans went crazy, shouting, "Sloopy! Sloopy!"

Problems have sometimes arisen because of the popularity of "Hang On Sloopy." In 1988, during the OSU/Syracuse game, the band was asked not to play the song because the press box and upper deck were shaking. Officials were afraid that the stands were not structurally sound enough to withstand the vibrations created by the fan enthusiasm. When Woody Hayes was still the coach, the fans could often be heard changing the words of the refrain to, "Hang on, Woody, Woody hang on!" Today, the original lyrics to the song are all but forgotten, except by

diehard fans, but
the refrain can always be heard reverberating through the Buckeye faithful.

The 116th General Assembly of the State of Ohio officially adopted "Hang On Sloopy" as the state rock and roll song. A copy of the official
declaration can be seen by visiting this site at the O-Zone. It's really quite funny. Don't miss it! "Hang On Sloopy" is now synonymous with Buckeye football and is the anthem of choice for many Ohio State fans." The Muck Fichigan website, http://members.aol.com/sloopyo/song.html.

[24] What'd I Say, p. 4.
[25] Ibid., p.7.
[26] Amazing Grace (Atlantic 1972).
[27] The Fillmore West was Graham's name for his venue in the Carousel Ballroom at Market and Van Ness Streets in San Francisco, after he had moved his shows from the Fillmore, a historic turn-of-the-century Italianate-style building that opened in 1910 at the corner of Fillmore and Geary Streets. Graham promoted shows at the Fillmore for two and a half years before moving to the larger venue that he dubbed "The Fillmore West."
    Graham opened The Fillmore East in 1967 in New York's Greenwich Village. Barely six weeks after the Aretha Franklin concert, Graham announced the closing of both venues in a long letter printed in The Village Voice.
[28] Graham recounted his greatest compliment when he overheard two young fans. One asked the other who the opening act was that night. The other replied, "It doesn't matter. It's the Fillmore."
[29] http://www.kendormusic.com/ensembles/19973.htm.
[30] Hinkley, D., "The Honker: King Curtis," New York Daily News, Nov. 1, 2004.
[31] "Curtis once estimated that he had backed more than 125 singers and musicians. They included the Shirelles, the

Coasters, Bobby Darin, Connie Francis, Nat "King" Cole, Sam Cooke, Wilson Pickett, Ray Charles, Andy Williams, Sam and Dave, Chuck Willis, Eric Clapton, the Allmans, and Delainey and Bonnie.{Not sure about these asterisks. Not conventional to use. Pls advise.} Curtis's talents encompassed every part of the record business. He could draw up a contract, make a deal, put a band together, or direct a recording session." <u>Rolling Stone,</u> September 16, 1971, p. 8.

[32] From a ministry founded by Father John Garcia Gensel in 1965, Saint Peter's established a jazz vespers service and organized outreach services to jazz musicians in need. That work continues today under Pastor Dale Lind.

[33] ". . . perfection is not what they're after. They're after something you want to listen to over and over again. So then we would work past the perfection point until it became natural, until it sounded almost improvised."— Dean Parks, session guitarist. <u>Steely Dan Aja</u> (Isis Productions & Eagle Rock Entertainment 1999).

[34] <u>Steely Dan Aja</u> (Isis Productions & Eagle Rock Entertainment 1999).
[35] http://www.kendormusic.com/ensembles/19973.htm.
[36] Ibid.
[37] ibid.
[38] Ibid.
[39] Ibid.
[40] MD 11/1992 {Please expand.}
[41] [Quote frm article]{Pls advise.}
[42] The Last Poets with Bernard Purdie, <u>Delights of the Garden</u> (1977), Casablanca or Celluloid labels.... {pls advise.}

According to Gil Scott-Heron, {should the following be in quotation marks?} the Last Poets were creating hip-hop before it was known that way—Just intense poetry over funky music. On this album the poets enlist the skills of jazz and funk drummer Bernard Purdie, one of the most recorded drummers of the last forty years. He's recorded for everybody from the Beatles to Coldcut, Aretha Franklin to James Brown, Herbie Hancock to Hall & Oates. On this one he is as tight as, well, I've never heard fills like this. The lyrics are woven in a dense political and metaphysical tapestry, and this is one to keep (belongs in that rare category of an album I can honestly say I need to have on both vinyl and CD, http://hiptingle.spydigital.com/index/forum/messages_display/9/Overlooked-Albums/Artists

[43] Louis Armstrong and Duke Ellington are famously quoted, saying that there are only two types of music—good or bad. Much of the resistance to category in art is to the commercial manipulation of categories solely for the purpose of selling artistic products.

[44] R. Jourdain Music, the Brain, and Ecstacy (William Morrow Publishing, 1997)

[45] Aja DVD.

[46] Mental imagery plays a critical role in performing music. When Purdie speaks of "seeing the music," he doesn't mean the individual notes of a score. The mental image of musical patterns that he perceives is broad, fluid, and nonlinear. He sees the entire piece in one view, as if viewing an abstract painting in relief. Those patterns don't conform to the marketing categories. There is no particular pattern for folk rock or country music. It's all music, and each composition is a separate challenge. In other words what he brings to the music is not a formula, but a vision. See Robert Jourdain, Music, the Brain, and Ecstacy (2002 Quill edition, originally published 1997 by William Morrow).

[47] Compiled from Carr, Fairweather & Priestley, Jazz: The Rough Guide (London 1995)

[48] Inclusion on Joel Whitburn Top 100 R&B Artist chart, based on highest chart position of singles. "Accompanied" includes both recording sessions and live performances.
[49] Compiled from Carr, Fairweather & Priestley, Jazz: The Rough Guide (London, 1995)
[50] Compiled from "The Soul Music Store Guide," 6/19/2003, www.soulmusic.com/newstoreguide.

Made in the USA
Columbia, SC
26 October 2022